Amassing Your Fortune After 40

ROBERT PASCUZZI AND STEVE SIEBOLD

DOWNLOAD FREE WORKBOOK:

www.RICHWORKBOOK.com

Also by the Authors

STEVE SIEBOLD

How Rich People Think

Secrets Self-Made Millionaires Teach Their Kids

177 Mental Toughness Secrets of the World Class

ROBERT PASCUZZI

Go 4 It!

The Ravine

GET TOUGH RETIRE RICH

Robert Pascuzzi and Steve Siebold

Published by
London House
www.londonhousepress.com

©2018 by London House Press

All Rights Reserved. Printed in the United States No part of this book may be reproduced, stored in or introduced into a retrieval system, or transmitted, in any form or by any means – electronic, mechanical, photocopying, recording or otherwise – without the prior written permission of the copyright owner.

ISBN: 978-0-9965169-3-8

TOC

Also by the Authors 3

Foreword 11

Introduction 13

A Message from the Authors 15

Chapter 1   Stop Screwing Around 17

Chapter 2   Don't Be a Putz 19

Chapter 3   Get Tough 21

Chapter 4   Start Killing It 23

Chapter 5   Don't be Greedy and Broke 25

Chapter 6   Stop Being Stupid 27

Chapter 7   Get Organized 29

Chapter 8   Don't Deviate 31

Chapter 9   Eradicate Magical Thinking 33

Chapter 10   Dump Approval Addiction 35

Chapter 11   Expect to Retire Rich 37

Chapter 12   Decide How Much is Enough 39

Chapter 13   Study Money 41

Chapter 14	Stop Procrastinating 43
Chapter 15	Think Big, Dream Bigger 45
Chapter 16	Get Fit 47
Chapter 17	Believe You Deserve It.. 49
Chapter 18	Be Optimistic and Pessimistic............................. 51
Chapter 19	Refuse to Settle.. 53
Chapter 20	Embrace Your Dream 55
Chapter 21	Craft Your Vision 57
Chapter 22	Cocoon Yourself 59
Chapter 23	Think for Yourself 61
Chapter 24	Embrace Critical Thinking.................................. 63
Chapter 25	Associate with Rich Retirees 65
Chapter 26	Listen to Your Heart/Act with Your Head 67
Chapter 27	Study Taxation 69
Chapter 28	Embrace Frugality 71
Chapter 29	Stop Apologizing... 73
Chapter 30	Employ Emotional Motivators 75
Chapter 31	Be Grateful 77
Chapter 32	Forgive Yourself 79
Chapter 33	Separate Logic and Emotion 81

Chapter 34	Invest in Your Interests 83
Chapter 35	Don't Count on Luck 85
Chapter 36	Enjoy the Ride 87
Chapter 37	Upgrade Your Beliefs 89
Chapter 38	Think Like a Comeback Artist 91
Chapter 39	Control Your Fear 93
Chapter 40	Sleep with One Eye Open 95
Chapter 41	Embrace the Suck of Investing 97
Chapter 42	Brush off the Losses 99
Chapter 43	Call on Your Courage 101
Chapter 44	Stay Excited 103
Chapter 45	Build Psychological Momentum 105
Chapter 46	Just Say No 107
Chapter 47	Seek Solitude 109
Chapter 48	Visualize Your Retirement 111
Chapter 49	Embrace Cause and Effect 113
Chapter 50	Study Markets 115
Chapter 51	Compartmentalize Your Emotions 117
Chapter 52	Expect a Fight 119
Chapter 53	Stop Keeping Up with the Joneses 121

Chapter 54	Be Doggedly Persistent 123
Chapter 55	Control Your Ego 125
Chapter 56	Embrace Boring Investments 127
Chapter 57	Build or Buy a Business 129
Chapter 58	Stop Tolerating Mediocrity 131
Chapter 59	Monitor Your Thinking and Language 133
Chapter 60	Build a Financial Team 135
Chapter 61	Study Personal Development 137
Chapter 62	Kill Bad Debt 139
Chapter 63	Stay Tough When You Lose 141
Chapter 64	Use Metacognition 143
Chapter 65	Control Your Self-Talk 145
Chapter 66	Study Experts 147
Chapter 67	Avoid Excessive Cognition 149
Chapter 68	Leverage Everything 151
Chapter 69	Don't Get Fancy 153
Chapter 70	Embrace Calculated Risk Taking 155
Chapter 71	Develop Sustained Concentration 157
Chapter 72	Build Your Strengths 159

Chapter 73	Be Decisive	161
Chapter 74	Don't Overreact	163
Chapter 75	Increase Your Financial Curiosity	165
Chapter 76	Maintain a Sense of Urgency	167
Chapter 77	Embrace Humor	169
Chapter 78	Go All In	171
Chapter 79	Sell, Baby, Sell!	173
Chapter 80	Join the Five O'clock Club	175
Chapter 81	Embrace Conflict	177
Chapter 82	Build Powerful Contacts	179
Chapter 83	Suspend Your Disbelief	181
Chapter 84	Learn to Choose	183
Chapter 85	Consider Constructive Criticism	185
Chapter 86	Rest Up	187
Chapter 87	Focus on the Future	189
Chapter 88	Avoid Middle-Class Thinking	191
Chapter 89	Expose Your Deepest Fear	193
Chapter 90	Bounce Back Strong	195
Chapter 91	Be Coachable	197

Chapter 92	Develop World-Class Investing Habits	199
Chapter 93	Study Investing Wisdom	201
Chapter 94	Be Humble	203
Chapter 95	Monitor Your Attitude	205
Chapter 96	Guard Your Energy	207
Chapter 97	Follow Your Gut	209
Chapter 98	Don't Be Afraid of Pain	211
Chapter 99	Never Say Die	213
Resources		217
The Authors		225

Foreword

I'm very enthusiastic about writing the foreword to this book, "Get Tough – Retire Rich." Years ago, I read where a Spanish distiller said, "The good life is expensive. There's another way to live that that doesn't cost as much, but it isn't any good." I can assure you, Robert Pascuzzi and Steve Siebold clearly understand how to live the good life. They're doing it and you can too when you internalize and act upon the ideas in this book. This book is a compilation of advice and strategies they know that work, not about stuff they've thought or heard about. To use a gambling analogy - these two guys are high rollers. The difference being, they're not gamblers, they're dealing with a sure thing. They're sure of the advice they're sharing because they both use it. It's proven and effective.

If you're into improving yourself you're probably familiar with the names Earl Nightingale, Larry Wilson, Bill Gove and Leland Val Van De Wall. Each of these men has left their earthly visit, but did so at the top of their game. They're known worldwide for having taught people how to live the good life. And, I might add, they were mentors of mine. Each one, in their own way, taught me how to pick the winner's in life and to develop the discipline to follow their direction.

Earl Nightingale said, "Experience is essential if you're going to win. You can either take a lifetime in getting the experience yourself or you can take the shortcut to success and benefit from the experience of others who have, proven by results, they know what they're doing. That's the route I took, and it helped me earn millions of dollars. All of the advice you require to get tough and retire rich is beautifully laid out in the pages of this book.

I value the friendship I've formed with Robert, Steve and their wives. They're ordinary guys who have achieved extraordinary results. Both really understand money: they know where it is, and they know how to get it. They know how to save it and how to enjoy it. They live a big life; the life most people merely dream about.

When I take an objective look at what each has accomplished, I'm reminded of an astronomer. Both have charted every move they've made. They're very articulate about laying it on the line. Not a lot of drama or fluff, just straight solid, advice that works ... every time ... for every person. When they say, "get tough," they mean it. Robert and Steve are mentally tough, but they're also very sophisticated, kind and understanding men. Though they're the kind of people you want to hang out with, rest assured they've got concrete advice I strongly recommend that you follow.

Make a decision, right here and now, that you're going to carry this book with you everywhere you go for the next two or three years. Commit to turning the wisdom from each powerful chapter into a habit ... into your habitual way of living. When you do that, strange and marvelous things will begin happening with constant regularity.

Bob Proctor
Master Success Coach and author of You Were Born Rich

Introduction

We live in a time where most Americans can't agree on just about anything. We can all agree on one thing though: we want to retire! Most of us spend more time working than we do with our family, at leisure or sleeping. And why do we do it? Some of us are fortunate to love what we do, but nearly all of us are working to provide for our needs, and the needs of those we love, both now and in the future.

But how much time do you actually spend planning to make sure you will have what you need in the future? The answer is simple: not enough. Most of us spend more time picking out a swimsuit than we do making sure we are on track to retire!

Not you though! You have already taken the first step towards financial independence. You took the time to purchase this book, and have actually started reading it. The first step towards financial independence is knowledge. The second is intelligent action. Bob and Steve give you the former in spades and all you need to take action as soon as your finish the last page.

There's a Chinese proverb that says 'The best time to plant a tree was yesterday. The second best time is today.' Grab your shovel. Let's go!

Peter Mallouuk, J.D., MBA, CFP
President & Chief Investment Officer
Creative Planning, Inc.

A Message from the Authors

The state of retirement in America is frightening. Most financial experts agree that your retirement savings should be at least 8 times your annual salary, but most people aren't saving enough. According to the Economic Policy Institute, mean retirement savings of a family 55 to 61 years old is $163,577. Most Americans will never be able to afford to retire. This is not only an individual problem – it's a national crisis. After all, how many 80-year-old greeters does Walmart need?

This problem is already bad, and it's getting worse. No one seems to be addressing the elephant in the room: as a country, what are we going to do with all of these old, poor people when they can't pay their bills? Are we going to let them starve in the street because they didn't save enough money? And if the government comes to their aid, how does that affect the people who diligently saved and invested their money? On top of these issues begs the question: if the government rescues these people, where will it get the money to do so?

These are problems of epic proportion, and there are no easy answers. This book will not speculate solutions. Our goal is to help to retire rich, so you can live out your golden years in the manner in which you desire and deserve. This book will be your roadmap to retiring rich by getting mentally tough, which means directing your psychological energy towards wealth and success while mastering your emotions.

Each short chapter is a directive designed to teach you the psychological tools, strategies and philosophies of the self-made rich. Our hope is that you will study the book, implement the ideas, and take action to secure your rich retirement.

We wish you the best of luck on your journey.

All the best,

Robert and Steve

Chapter 1

Stop Screwing Around

Today is the day to start saving and investing. How long have you been promising yourself that you'd start socking more money away for retirement? No matter how long you've waited, don't feel badly. Most people have little savings, even in their 50s and 60s.

The best day to start saving and investing is yesterday. The second best time is today. No matter how much or little you can afford, the key is to start investing a portion of your income right now. Even if it's only 1% of each paycheck, the habit of consistent saving and investing is the secret to retiring rich. Our opening message is bold: stop screwing around and start getting serious about your retirement. This isn't a game – it's your life. It's one thing to be young and broke, and quite another to be old and broke. It's nasty scenario, and only money can solve it. This is why you must take action today, not tomorrow, and begin the journey to securing your retirement. Force yourself to take a small amount of money, no matter how insignificant, and invest it. I'm not talking about gambling in the Wall Street casino or speculating with complex financial products. I'm talking about beefing up your savings account, reducing your debt or selling off unwanted assets and possessions. Everything counts, even if it seems too small to make a difference. The changes don't always appear in your checking account or on your balance sheet. More often they occur in the deep recesses of your mind, where your new habits are slowly taking hold and changing the way your brain is wired around money. Retiring rich starts in your mind, not in your wallet.

> "If you want to be wealthy, live below your means."
> — *Paul Merriman*

CRITICAL THINKING QUESTION

Would setting aside 1% of your income seriously impact your budget?

ACTION STEP

Make a decision to save and invest at least 1% of your income for the rest of your career.

Chapter 2

Don't Be a Putz

No one is coming to the rescue. You are the only person who can take control of your money. Financial advisors, brokers, TV pundits and other professionals can offer guidance, advice and support, but no one can do it for you. This is your responsibility. If you're married, then it's also your spouse's responsibility. You must be tough enough to change your habits and start the process. The good news is that the hardest part is the first investment. Once you're in the game, even if you start with $10 dollars, you'll begin building psychological momentum. Don't allow yourself to procrastinate. Only a fool believes that he'll change tomorrow what he refuses to change today. Stop lying to yourself about how you're going to start saving when you have more money. Your income only determines the amount you invest, but the bigger issue is the act of investing any amount. The real danger is not in others deceiving you about money, it's in deceiving yourself. It's easy to tell yourself that you'll start saving someday, when you're older, after you have kids, when the kids are grown, when you get a raise or a better job, or when you start that new business.

Again, if you've used any of these excuses in the past, you're not alone. Most of us have done the same thing and made the same excuses. The secret is to start moving forward by taking some kind of action, no matter how seemingly insignificant.

> "One of the dumbest things you can do with your money is spend it."
>
> — *Robert Wilson*

CRITICAL THINKING QUESTION

"Have you fallen into the psychological trap of believing that saving tomorrow will be easier than saving today?"

ACTION STEP

Start taking full responsibility for your financial future by making a proactive effort towards it every day.

Chapter 3

Get Tough

Mental toughness is the ability to control and manipulate your emotions, especially under pressure. As an investor with the goal of retiring rich, mental toughness will be critical to your success. The first part of the process is discipline, specifically as it relates to your financial goals. It's easy to spend money, and it's fun. Spending gives us instant gratification, which is far more attractive than the boring and banal acts of saving and investing. It's a dull process that lasts for years without a payoff, and that keeps many people from engaging. This is where mental toughness kicks in. If you're going to retire rich, you must learn to deny yourself the immediate pleasure of spending in exchange for the peace of mind of having money in the bank. This requires you to make a decision – an adult decision – to serve your long-term best interests. It doesn't take mental toughness to buy things, but it takes mental toughness not to buy things. It requires self-control, a skill you acquire through practice. No one wants to employ self-control, because we prefer to feel good. This leads us down a path of failure and frustration. It's like waking up early to exercise. Few of us enjoy it. When the alarm goes off, the bed feels like the greatest place on earth. The temperature is perfect, pillows are puffed and all you want to do is close your eyes and go back to sleep. And that's what fat, out-of-shape people do. Meanwhile, the fit people bounce out of bed and head to the gym. Only mental toughness will make you do that, and if you're going to retire rich, that's what you will have to do.

> "The definition of discipline is giving yourself a command then following it."
>
> *— Bob Proctor*

CRITICAL THINKING QUESTION

If you were on trial for being mentally tough, would there be enough evidence to convict you?

ACTION STEP

Set a goal to become more mentally tough by adding more discipline to your daily routine.

RECOMMENDED RESOURCE

<u>177 Mental Toughness Secrets of the World Class</u>
By Steve Siebold

Chapter 4

Start Killing It

If you want to retire rich, the worst thing you can do is play it safe. I'm not encouraging you to invest in risky things or to try to time the market. These are bad strategies employed by naïve people. What I'm referring to is making a do-or-die commitment to your ultimate retirement goal. Make a decision to do whatever it takes. If you need help, get it. If you decide to do it yourself, study it. If you want to implement some combination of the two, be sure to do your homework. 'Killing it' in this context means taking control of yourself and your money, even if you're being guided by an outside expert. The more you dive into the savings and investment game, the more you'll begin to enjoy it. Refuse to be intimidated by complex investments and gray haired experts. Your goal is to retire rich, not to become a Wall Street titan. Unless you're managing someone else's money, you only have to become proficient in overseeing your own retirement, and that means it must be based on the retirement lifestyle that you wish to enjoy. It's your sole responsibility to start, grow and protect your retirement fund. There are lots of honest, competent, hardworking fiduciaries out there to assist you, yet no one will ever watch your money as closely as you. Educate yourself a little every day, and within a few years, you will have developed enough expertise to know when a professional is giving you sound advice or suggesting a product that's loaded with fees and commissions. Once you have a firm grasp on the specific investments that match your tolerance for risk and your long-term goals, you'll be on your way to a rich retirement.

"The difference between a rich investor and a poor investor is the quality – and timeliness – of his information."

— John Cassidy

CRITICAL THINKING QUESTION

Have you made a serious decision to do whatever it takes to retire rich?

ACTION STEP

Set a goal to read four investment books in the next 12 months.

Chapter 5

Don't be Greedy and Broke

Professional speculators take huge risks to produce large gains. This is the professional gamblers mentality. Though many of these people are well-educated individuals with a track record of success, they often end up broke. The professional gambler is always in search of the quick buck. This is not for you. As sexy as speculation sounds, few have the talent to beat the market. Fast and fat gains are rooted in greed, and greed has a way of wiping out retirement funds.

When it comes to money, safe is the new sexy. You don't need to earn exorbitant interest rates to retire rich. What you need are safe, steady investments that provide a reasonable rate of return while protecting your principal. Don't expect this strategy to make the news or be the topic of conversation at your next cocktail party. It's not flashy, and it's unlikely to impress your neighbors. It's simply a sound strategy that, combined with time and tax deferred interest, will help your retirement fund grow. Contrary to what you read in the papers, when it comes to investing, not everyone is breaking the bank. While the headlines love to show Gordon Gekko driving his Rolls Royce through the gates of his mansion, most real-life millionaires are driving 10-year-old pick up trucks into their modest, middle class, paid-for, homes.

> "Be fearful when others are greedy, and greedy when others are fearful."
>
> — *Warren Buffett*

CRITICAL THINKING QUESTION

"How much money is enough for you to retire rich?"

ACTION STEP

Set a goal to calculate exactly how much money you'll need in retirement, add 25%, and then build a plan to attain it.

Chapter 6

Stop Being Stupid

In December 2017, a USA Today poll reported that the median savings balance among working households in the United States for people aged 50-55, was $8,000. And if you think that's bad, try this: for those aged 56-61, the median savings balance is $17,000. The study goes on to say that by age 55, you should have 7 times your annual income stashed away in a 401k or IRA.

This is a pipe dream for most, but it's also solid math. Odds are you're going to live into your 80s, and possibly your 90s. The advances in modern medicine, combined with healthy lifestyle choices, means there's a strong chance that most people would live 30-40 years in retirement. While that's good news, it also means you're going to need 30-40 years of money to fund that second lifetime.

So what's changed in society since our parent's retirement days? In a word, everything. Pensions are gone. Retirement contributions are optional. And easy credit has people purchasing things they can't afford. So like it or not, you are now your own Chief Financial Officer. You're on your own. And if you're not growing your nest egg, it's time to get tough. Stop spending today and ignoring tomorrow. That being said, if you're guilty of this, don't beat yourself up. Most of us are. It's fun to spend money. The problem is that the most important aspect of growing money is time, especially when growing your retirement money tax deferred. The best thing you can do is forgive yourself for acting stupid and make a decision to join the ranks of the boring, consistent investors who quietly build their fortune undeterred by the allure of the latest indulgence.

> "When everybody is thinking the same way, nobody is thinking."
>
> — *General George Patton*

CRITICAL THINKING QUESTION

Are you ready to get serious about retiring rich and commit to a plan of action?

> **ACTION STEP**
>
> Give yourself 90-days to construct a comprehensive retirement plan. If you need help, pay for it.

RECOMMENDED RESOURCE

People Are Idiots and I Can Prove It
By Larry Winget

Chapter 7

Get Organized

Start thinking about how you want to live, and what you want to do when you retire. It may be many years from now, and your dreams may be different, but your planning begins today. Everything you want comes with a price tag, and inflation will only increase these costs. Start by making a list of where you want to live and what you want to do. And if you don't know, guess. You can always adjust your plans. The earlier you begin, the more likely you are to make it. And if you're 40 or older, you have no time to lose.

Start organizing your thoughts. If you're married or coupled, talk it though with your partner. Financial organization begins with psychological organization. Vow to hash out every detail, and don't forget to consider the financial implications. These include the fees and other costs of your investments. Take everything you can think of into consideration, and if you need help, find a trusted fiduciary and pay him or her for their time and expertise. Hiring an expert with nothing to gain but an hourly fee is an intelligent way to get unbiased advice. Ask family, friends and colleagues if they can recommend potential candidates. As in any profession, the quality of advice can vary substantially. People can only offer you what they know, and all advisors are not created equal. Performing your due diligence will yield stronger advice and a better nights sleep. Once you've been advised, organize your financial plan to match your current vision of your retirement, knowing that this will likely change every few years as your life and desires evolve.

"For every minute spent in organizing, an hour is earned."

— *Ben Franklin*

CRITICAL THINKING QUESTION

On a scale of 1-7, with 7 being most organized, how would you rate yourself?

ACTION STEP

Get 5 recommendations for financial advisors from trusted family, friends and colleagues, and interview each one to ensure the best fit for you.

Chapter 8

Don't Deviate

Setting goals, planning outcomes and organizing action steps are simple, logical, linear processes. They require time, energy and effort. But as with most logic-based work, that's the easiest variable in the equation. The tough part is sticking to the plan while refusing to deviate from the course you've charted. The financial desires of the present are an ongoing, omnipresent threat. It's easy to spend today instead of saving for tomorrow. This is why you must rely on your emotional muscle to keep you on course, headed toward the Promised Land.

Mental toughness is the secret to staying on course, and this includes abandoning your safety plan in pursuit of sexier, more potentially profitable investments. Is betting on the latest tech stock more fun than you're boring old fixed indexed annuity or mutual fund? Probably. Yet the money you have in the annuity or mutual fund is safe and the returns are reasonable. The tech stock you're dying to buy might be off the board in 12 months. If you can afford the risk and have the stomach to endure large losses, you may consider high-risk investments. But for most of us, our best plan to is keep our money safely tucked away, growing steadily, gracefully navigating the natural swings and shifts in the market.

Don't get sucked into the hysteria of huge gains about which people brag. Refuse to get caught up in the feeling that everyone is getting rich in the market while you're sitting on the sidelines with your safe little nest egg. It's worth recalling that in the days of the gold rush, most of the people who got rich were the ones selling the shovels.

"It's often a long road to quick profits."

— *Humphrey Neill*

CRITICAL THINKING QUESTION

Are you ready to stick to your retirement plan for the long-term?

ACTION STEP

Decide today to construct your plan and stay the course, regardless of how tempted you are to deviate.

RECOMMENDED RESOURCE

Unshakeable

By Tony Robbins

Chapter 9

Eradicate Magical Thinking

Growing up emotionally is one of the toughest aspects of life, yet it's necessary to retiring rich. This means grounding your thoughts, actions and strategies in critical thinking. American society has an affinity for magical, mystical thinking, which is why more socially sophisticated countries tend to marginalize our culture. Despite our immaturity, our country continues to be successful as well as feared, due to our wealth and military power.

Getting rich requires reality-based thinking, specifically as it relates to saving, investing and self-discipline. Our emotionally charged society wants you to believe that flashy material possessions make you successful, when the fact is that most of these things are wealth draining, non-income producing, over-priced toys. That's how Madison Avenue became so rich. They painted the picture that sports cars and big homes made you successful, and once the public believed it, they sold them these items at inflated prices. People don't overextend themselves for things; they overextend themselves for the emotional feeling they believe they'll experience when they acquire these things. It's a world-class marketing scheme, and if you're going to retire rich, you must avoid it like the plague. Instead, focus your critical thinking on acquiring income-producing assets like rental property; equities that pay dividends, and businesses that generate positive cash flow.

Never get emotional or think magically about money. Emotion clouds judgment, and successful investing requires good judgment. As soon as you find yourself becoming emotionally attached to an investment, walk away. Obsession leads to irrational exuberance, over valuation and losing money. Refuse to get caught up in an asset's emotional allure. You will always have another opportunity to acquire income-producing assets at the right price, because there will always be emotionally-driven sellers who are forced to liquidate.

> "Don't feel, think!"
>
> — *Ayn Rand*

CRITICAL THINKING QUESTION

When it comes to saving and investing money, how often do you allow emotion to cloud your judgment?

ACTION STEP

Practice making non-emotional decisions that serve your best interests.

Chapter 10

Dump Approval Addiction

Human beings are genetically predisposed to seek approval.

100,000 plus years ago, people lived in tribes, and each member relied on the others for food, shelter and protection. If you didn't have the approval of the tribe, your family starved to death. It was a simple and profound reality. Since then our genetics have evolved to include the need for approval, though in modern times we don't require it for survival. When we're children, we seek approval from parents, teachers, coaches, and other adults of influence, and when we get it, we tend to get what we want. In other words, it works. This reinforces this genetically driven desire and makes it stronger, so by the time we become adults, we are full-blown approval addicts. Most of us continue through life unaware of this debilitating, emotional addiction. We manifest it in a number of ways, including getting a college degree in order to please our parents, accepting a job we don't like because it looks good, and making high-risk investments to impress our friends. Buying shares of a blue chip company, no matter how over-valued, makes better country club conversation than purchasing a broken down duplex. The secret is to stop caring about what others think, and make retiring rich your primary goal. Besides being a distraction, the fact is that people don't spend much time thinking about us. They are far more concerned with their own wellbeing, as they should be.

> "Care about what others think and you will always be their prisoner."
>
> — *Lao Tzu*

CRITICAL THINKING QUESTION

On a scale of 1-7, with 7 being most addicted, how addicted are you to the approval of others?

ACTION STEP

Make a decision to stop worrying about what other people think about your actions.

Chapter 11

Expect to Retire Rich

When it comes managing your portfolio, your expectations will determine your actions. Studies show that most people expect to struggle through life, including retirement. This is a mistake, as positive expectation is the catalyst of retiring rich. After all, if you don't think it's possible to retire rich, why bother trying? The fact is that most people are not trying, and their lack of effort towards this monumental goal is rooted in more than laziness. To the contrary, most people aren't lazy. If the average person were convinced that he actually had a chance to retire rich, he'd spend less time on the couch and more time planning his victory. Most people's grand expectations are squashed early in life, never to be cultivated or considered again. The good news is that expectations are manufactured in the mind, and they can be upgraded and altered. If you're reading this book, odds are you expect to retire rich. People who expect to struggle rarely study, as reading tends to interfere with watching sports, reality shows and playing video games.

We want to challenge you to raise your already high level of expectation even higher. Whatever amount of money with which you expect to retire, double it. We know that's a tall order, and maybe one you believe is impossible. But millions of people do it every day, and it all starts with telling yourself that you are going to make it happen. The mind is a machine that can be manipulated to serve your best interests, and this is something of which you need to take advantage.

"High expectations are the key to everything."

— *Sam Walton*

CRITICAL THINKING QUESTION

Do you expect to retire rich?

> **ACTION STEP**
>
> Start telling yourself everyday that you expect to retire rich.

Chapter 12

Decide How Much is Enough

While everyone agrees that more money is better than less, you need to decide on a figure. Some people need five million and others, five billion. Rich is a relative term, and your job is to figure out how it relates to you. How much money would be enough to do anything you want for 30-40 years? Do you have beer or champagne taste? Are you planning on traveling the world by private jet or playing shuffleboard in your backyard? Everyone is different, and there are no right or wrong answers. It's your life and your retirement, and you're only going to get one shot. Take inventory of your deepest desires, and if you're married or coupled, be sure to include your partner. Take into consideration that since you're discussing something that will take place many years in the future, it can be difficult to speculate how your desires may evolve. That's okay. The main thing is not to let this uncertainty stop you from getting started. Remember that you can always change it. The key is to get an initial idea and cost estimate on paper. This will create psychological momentum, and it will keep you focused on your savings and investment plan. Once you list all of the things you'd like to do, assign an initial cost estimate, including inflation and a 10% margin for error. In other words, if you decide that you'll need $10 million, add 10% and make it $11 million. This will cover unanticipated costs and unexpected events. Once you decide how much is enough, you can move towards acquiring the exact amount with peace of mind.

> "The American Dream is independence, and being able to create that dream for yourself."
>
> — *Marsha Blackburn*

CRITICAL THINKING QUESTION

Do you know exactly how much money you'll need to retire rich?

ACTION STEP

Calculate how much money you will need to retire based on the level of lifestyle you want to live.

STARTLING STATISTIC

50% of all American's have less than $10,000 in savings. (2018)

Chapter 13

Study Money

Gone are the days of trusting your money with an advisor prior to educating yourself. It's an old, but true axiom: no one will ever watch your money like you. If you're going to retire rich, it's imperative that you study money and everything related to it. Yes, it takes time and effort, and for some people the lessons don't come easy. The good news is that, thanks to the Internet, access to information is abundant. The web is packed with millions of educational videos, audios, blogs, articles, white papers and podcasts. Best of all, they're free. All that's required is an investment of time and energy. You should also study the numerous financial instruments, contracts and vehicles. The average investor is ignorant about how most wealth building tools work, and that ignorance costs them a fortune. Financial product creators are masters at burying fees, and sometimes these fees in addition to inflation can eat away and even exceed the gains that the product produces. This is the dirty little secret of the financial services industry, and it creates a case of 'buyer-beware.' Savvy investors discipline themselves to build study time into their daily routine, and in a relatively short time, they learn how to guide their financial advisor in the direction that best matches their goals and dreams.

Set aside 15 to 30 minutes a day, preferably in the early morning when your brain is at its best, to read, listen or watch educational offerings around money. You may be surprised at how quickly you begin to see the big picture for your retirement plan. Financial concepts and strategies that previously intimidated you begin to unfold and become simplified. You'll not only become a better investor, you'll also experience a peaceful, easy feeling knowing that you are now in full control of your financial future.

> "You need at least seven times your annual salary to retire."
>
> — *Randy Neuman*

CRITICAL THINKING QUESTION

Are you investing as much time studying money as you are watching your favorite television show?

ACTION STEP

Invest 15 to 30 minutes per day studying anything related to money that can help you become a better investor, and keep a written log of your progress.

STARTLING STATISTIC:

28% of American's over 55 have no retirement savings.

Chapter 14

Stop Procrastinating

We're all guilty of it from time to time. We put off things that should be done today for tomorrow, the next day, or even forever. This is fine when it comes to building a new tool shed in the backyard, but when it comes to your money, it's financial suicide. Time is your retirement money's best friend, and the longer you wait to save, invest and educate yourself, the less chance you have of retiring rich. The compound interest clock is always ticking, the only question is, is it ticking in your favor?

Most investors start way too late to plan for their golden years. After all, it's easier to wait than it is to get started. When you're in your 20s, it's easy to convince yourself that you'll never get old. It seems so far away. On top of this delusion is the fact that most of us struggle to pay our bills when we enter the workforce, and it often gets tougher as we marry and have children. Where is all of this extra money supposed to come from? When you can barely meet your monthly expenses and you're fighting with your partner over every penny, it's easy to ignore an event that will happen 50 years in the future. This is a formula for disaster. The effects of compound interest over a three to five decade span can be substantial, and it's worth every sacrifice to take full advantage of it. If you're reading this at 40, 50 or 60, don't be discouraged. Yes, you've lost a lot of time, but you can still retire rich if you get started now and you embrace an aggressive, pro-active approach. Make a commitment to start today and you'll quickly move closer to the retirement life you desire.

> "Procrastination is like a credit card. It's a lot of fun until you get the bill."
>
> — *Christopher Parker*

CRITICAL THINKING QUESTION

On a scale of 1-7, with 7 being most, how often do you procrastinate when it comes to working toward your retirement goals?

ACTION STEP

Set a goal to take at least one action per day that moves you closer towards retiring rich.

Chapter 15

Think Big, Dream Bigger

When it comes to retirement, most people take a minimalist approach. They envision their twilight years as being low income, reduced expenses and a frugal lifestyle. But what if it didn't have to be this way? What if you could reimagine your retirement as a time of abundance, luxury and even excess? After all, some people do retire rich, albeit a small percentage of the population. The point is that it's possible, and that's what this book is about.

The first step is to push yourself to think bigger as it relates to your retirement. Instead of the mass mentality game of survival, embrace the idea that you might be able to live out the final chapter of your life in the lap of luxury. But what if you're starting late, like most of us, and you're more concerned about having enough to retire than you are about the lifestyle you want to live? This is where most people spend their thinking time, in a low vibrational level of fear and scarcity. The problem is thoughts of fear and scarcity breed even more thoughts of fear and scarcity. The thought frequency in which you spend the most time will organically attract more thoughts at that level. Although this idea may sound ethereal or even mystical, it's actually the nature of how mental energy proliferates. This is why negative people are attracted to negative people, while positive people are attracted to positive people. It's not personality; it's energy. The energy of envisioning a survival-based retirement will attract investment strategies that match this low level energy.

All that's required to move in the opposite direction is simply thinking about retiring rich, with an abundance of money and resources. This high level energy will attract investments and strategies that will lead you toward that outcome.

"You have to think big to be big."

— *Claude W. Bristol*

CRITICAL THINKING QUESTION

Are you thinking big enough to retire rich?

> **ACTION STEP**
>
> Make a list of the 10 biggest thinkers you know or have ever heard of, and read their books, watch their interviews or attend one of the their public events.

Chapter 16

Get Fit

We've all heard it before: a fit body leads to a fit mind. This adage has been handed down through the ages, and it's true. This is why to retire rich, you must put your body in the best shape of your life. If you're overweight, go on a diet. If you're eating habits are poor, change them. If you smoke three packs of cigarettes a day, quit smoking. Extreme success requires extreme habits, and your body is no exception. The more energy you have, the better you will feel and the more mental clarity you will experience.

Now to be clear, we're not talking about taking up Mixed Martial Arts or running a marathon. The word extreme is a relative term, and in this context we mean extreme compared to the average, overweight couch potatoes that make up 70 percent of society. If you want to train to climb Mount Everest or compete in the Iron Man, more power to you. We're only suggesting moderate exercise, better food choices and a healthy body weight. If you're already in great shape, you can skip the rest of this chapter. If not, today is the day to get started. The good news is it won't take long to gain momentum, and the closer you get to your fitness goals, the better you will feel. Remember that we are all products of our daily habits, and every new habit starts with the first step. Set a goal to take one action step each day toward building physical habits that will empower your body and energize your mind.

"The reason I exercise is for the quality of life I enjoy."

— *Kenneth Cooper*

CRITICAL THINKING QUESTION

How would you classify your current level of fitness: poor, good or great?

ACTION STEP

Schedule a physical with your doctor and determine your ideal weight.

STARTLING STATISTIC

160 million American's are either overweight or obese.

Chapter 17

Believe You Deserve It

If you live and work in free market economy, and you're able to serve enough people to generate a fortune, you deserve to be rich. If you're savvy enough to manage your money and discipline yourself to save, invest and grow it over time, you deserve to be rich. If you're willing to take the time and make the necessary effort to educate yourself on the opportunities and pitfalls of all things financial, and you act on that education, you deserve to be rich.

Some people feel undeserving of wealth. Sometimes it's out of guilt for making more money than their hardworking, underpaid parents. Other times they compare their good fortune to the poverty of the third world.

These are examples of beliefs that hold people back from retiring rich, and they are both meritless and illogical. Consider this ideology: life isn't fair. The world isn't fair. Money isn't fair. Throughout the history of the world, life has never been fair and never will be. The question is not one of fairness, greed or guilt, but what do any of these things have to do with you? Shouldn't we all attempt to make the most of the opportunities with which we are presented? If the 70-year-old man living in poverty in a poor Indian village had the opportunity to retire rich, do you think he would take it? In addition, if you have the chance to retire rich, don't you owe it to everyone that doesn't have that opportunity to capitalize on it? Never allow the middle-class brainwashing of your past to get in the way of your abundant future. Tell yourself that you deserve to be rich, and then move toward this goal boldly and fearlessly, like a thundering locomotive steaming down the track.

> "If you deserve it, go get it."
>
> — *Conor McGregor*

CRITICAL THINKING QUESTION

What would you have to do to believe that you deserve to be rich?

ACTION STEP

Write down three steps that you need to take to strengthen your belief that you deserve to be rich.

Chapter 18

Be Optimistic and Pessimistic

Positive thinking is a beautiful thing. It makes us feel good, directs our thoughts toward uplifting stories and events, and helps us see the upside of negative experiences. Being an optimist delivers similar benefits, including boosting our emotions and immune systems. There is almost universal agreement on the healthy nature of both of these inspiring psychological approaches to life and living.

On the other hand, negative thinking has been demonized for generations. Negative thinkers are frowned upon, as are pessimists who use fear and doubt as a strategy. In order to increase your odds of retiring rich, it's prudent to utilize both negative and positive thinking, as well as optimism and pessimism. Positive thinking will keep you feeling good and moving forward. Optimism will help you maintain hope. On the opposite side of the spectrum, negative thinking will help you maintain a healthy, objective balance to ensure you don't fall into a delusional level of magical, wishful thinking. There are lots of solid, stable investments of which you can take advantage, and there are also lots of scams and poor investments that can steal every penny you've ever earned. There are brilliant, honest, dedicated fiduciaries that will always serve your best interests, and there are greedy salespeople and brokers that base their recommendations on products that pay large commissions. The challenge is differentiating between the two.

The world is both a beautiful and brutal place, and human beings are both honest and corrupt. To retire rich, be sure to keep your chin up and your eyes open. Have faith in those who educate and advise you, but be sure to check the silverware before they leave.

....

"The pessimist complains about the wind. The optimist expects it to change. The realist adjusts the sail."

— *William A. Ward*

....

CRITICAL THINKING QUESTION

When it comes to retiring rich, are you more optimistic or pessimistic?

ACTION STEP

Write down three reasons that you are optimistic about retiring rich, and three reasons that you are pessimistic.

RECOMMENDED RESOURCE

Learned Optimism
By Dr. Martin E.P. Seligman

Chapter 19

Refuse to Settle

You only get one shot at retirement. No do-overs. That's why it's critical that you don't settle for anything less than retiring rich. After all, if you have a chance to do something few people ever have, why would you aim for less than the best?

Refusing to settle is no guarantee that you'll be able to manifest your ultimate dream, but it certainly puts you in the game. Once you settle for less, you have raised the white flag of surrender and informed the universe that you are willing to be happy with whatever life hands you. While this may be every psychologists dream strategy for peace and happiness, it's clearly an act of capitulation. People who retire rich aren't always the ones you'd expect. Of course you expect the multimillionaire with more money than he knows what to do with to retire rich. Outside of doing something foolish with their wealth, these people are almost guaranteed to live out their golden years in abundance. But there are a percentage of people who struggle their entire lives, and in the last few years before retirement, hit a financial home run. These are people who typically started saving late in life. Many of them were building businesses and reinvesting everything they had, in terms of both time and money, always believing they would be able to cash in someday. They drove Fords instead of Ferraris and they lived in modest homes in middle-class neighborhoods. America is full of these people, and while they always appeared to be settling, what they were really doing was preparing themselves for their one swing at their own home run. The fact is that everyone who aspires to retire rich is in a different position, but no matter how far ahead or behind you are; you'll always have a chance if you refuse to settle.

"You are what you settle for."

— *Janis Joplin*

CRITICAL THINKING QUESTION

Do your efforts towards your retirement indicate that you are playing to win or settling for less?

ACTION STEP

Imagine yourself, years from now in retirement, having settled. How does it make you feel?

RECOMMENDED RESOURCE

You're Broke Because You Want To Be
By Larry Winget

Chapter 20

Embrace Your Dream

What does your dream retirement look like? Have you thought about what the ultimate scenario might entail? Do you see yourself lying on a beach in Latin America sipping rum out of a coconut, or living in downtown New York doing volunteer work?

Whatever your dream, you must embrace it wholeheartedly if you want to have a chance to see it through. The more vivid and detailed the dream, the easier it is to implant it into your subconscious mind. The beauty of embedding your vision in the deep recesses of your mind is that you will automatically begin to move toward the picture with the strongest emotional charge. The longer the pictures develop in your mind, the clearer they become and the more real they will seem. Eventually your dream will begin to feel as if it's already a reality. Any feelings of overwhelm, fear or intimidation will subside as your mind becomes accustomed to the new pictures, or more accurately, the perception of your new reality. This process is the purposeful manipulation of your emotions, and while it can sound ethereal, our emotional nature makes it real. As emotional creatures, human beings are susceptible to grand delusions and massive leaps of magical thinking. As a macro example, there are over 4,000 religions in the world, collectively representing thousands of gods, and they cannot all be true. As a matter of fact, there's little proof that any of them are true. But that doesn't stop billions of people from believing in these supernatural beings, even in the face of 21st century science.

Our point is not anti-religion. Our point is that human beings will believe anything that is embedded into their minds that is charged with emotion. When it comes to your retirement dream, the emotional charge should be the overwhelming excitement, pleasure and life satisfaction you will experience. Use this knowledge to manipulate your emotions and move closer to your ultimate vision.

"So many of our dreams at first seem impossible, then they seem improbable, and then, when we summon the will, they will soon become inevitable."

— *Christopher Reeve*

CRITICAL THINKING QUESTION

What does your dream retirement look and feel like?

ACTION STEP

List the three aspects of your retirement dream that give you the strongest emotional charge.

Chapter 21

Craft Your Vision

Part of getting tough is getting specific, and when it comes to retiring rich, that means crafting the nitty-gritty details of your ultimate retirement. If the dream drives emotion, then the vision drives the details. This means dissecting every piece of your retirement future, from where you will live to how you will live. Are you going to live a retirement village in Florida, an independent living community in Arizona or beachfront mansion in Laguna? Think of the vision as a lifestyle business plan that includes every aspect you can think of, knowing that you can make changes and updates as the years draw closer.

Your vision should be a comprehensive written document that details everything you wish to imagine doing. An example might be taking up scuba diving, calligraphy or gardening, even if you've never considered these activities in the past. You're creating a document that's flexible and fluid, meaning it can be altered at any time. The strategy behind creating something that will likely be drastically different by the time it's implemented is to start the process of moving toward the future. Just like creating a business plan years before the business is launched, it includes projections, speculation and outright guesses. Every banker that's ever evaluated a business plan knows that the purpose of the process is to show clear direction based on the current information available. The vision directs your mind to begin moving forward towards the pictures that are created from the details in the document. It also gives you an idea of how much the vision will cost to create and maintain, which will help you determine your long-term investment strategy. Begin crafting your vision for the future today, and with each new detail you describe, you will feel a sense of excitement and anticipation.

"Vision without execution is just hallucination."

— *Henry Ford*

CRITICAL THINKING QUESTION

Does your written vision include the necessary detail?

ACTION STEP

List every detail of your retirement knowing you can always change or adjust them whenever necessary.

Chapter 22

Cocoon Yourself

The simple fact that you're reading this book separates you from the masses. This is not a motivational sound bite, but a statistical reality. While you're studying strategies on how to retire rich, most people are playing video games, watching TV, tail gating, or engaging in some other menial pursuit. This is not a put down to the average person – it's simply the way it is. It's one of the foundational reasons that the rich get richer and the poor, poorer. While they're playing, you're working.

Beyond giving yourself the proverbial pat on the back, consider cocooning your consciousness from the masses. Cocooning is a method of building an imaginary protective cocoon around your consciousness by limiting your exposure to middle-class thinkers. The purpose is simple: to insulate yourself from the highly contagious fear and scarcity-based mindset. Contrary to the way this strategy has been demonized as elitism, the truth is that cocooning is a defensive strategy designed to protect love and abundance-based thinking from being eroded by fear and scarcity- based thoughts, habits, actions and philosophies. Cocooning may be controversial, and it may even cost you a few friends, but it's critical that you employ it as part of your strategy.

Replace spending time with fear-based people by surrounding yourself with big thinkers doing great things. Your goal should be to start out as the smallest thinker in the group, and once you've raised your level of thinking to match the top of group, move on to a group where you're once again the smallest thinker. This will guarantee that your thinking and expectations will continue to expand and grow.

> "Surround yourself with only people who are going to lift you higher."
>
> — *Oprah Winfrey*

CRITICAL THINKING QUESTION

Are the people in your inner circle helping or hurting you?

ACTION STEP

List three people you'd like to have in your inner circle.

Chapter 23

Think for Yourself

The world is full of followers. Most people prefer to be told what to do and how to do it, rather than having to think for themselves. To some degree, we are all products of other people's thinking, mainly because we are indoctrinated with their thinking as children. Whether it's in school, sports, church, scouts, neighborhoods, clubs and other places of influence, we are brainwashed before we are cognitively capable of knowing it.

Now to be fair, some of the thinking we learn is useful and good. It certainly helps to know how to read and write, and to keep our hands to ourselves and respect others. The danger lies in the false narratives, especially the ones that teach us to follow blindly. Most of us spend are entire childhood being taught what to think instead of how to think, which is why the system produces more sheep than shepherds. For most of us, independent thinking must be learned, and it's often an uphill battle protested by the people closest to us. Retiring rich is a prime example: it's a concept that most people see as rooted in greed. The masses make sense of the world through the indoctrination in which they were raised, and anything that disrupts their worldview is often met with fear, anger and belligerence. This is why you can't discuss sex, politics or religion in mixed company. Many people are incapable of separating their emotions from objective facts, which means disagreement's can quickly escalate into attacks.

Thinking for yourself is not encouraged in most cultures, only in places where education is emphasized. This is why college campuses have always been incubators for independent thinking, as have think tanks like the Aspen Institute. Thinking for yourself may not make you popular, but it will definitely help you retire rich.

"Take the risk of thinking for yourself."

— *Christopher Hitchens*

CRITICAL THINKING QUESTION

When it comes to your retirement, are you thinking for yourself?

ACTION STEP

Ask your best friend if they consider you to be someone who thinks for yourself.

Chapter 24

Embrace Critical Thinking

Critical thinking means making decisions based on greater criteria devoid of emotion. It's seeing the world as it is, as opposed to what we wish it were. Sometimes reality beats fantasy, but most times the opposite is true.

Learning to employ critical thinking is as easy as challenging common statements and so called conventional wisdom. For example, how many times have your heard the idea that the world is a wonderful place? Lots of times, right? Well, critical thinking would tell us that the world is a wonderful place, if you're among the minority of the populous that reside in wealthy countries. When 3 billion people live on less than two dollars a day and a child staves to death every seven seconds, it's hard to make the case that the world is a wonderful place. Another example is the widely held belief that money is difficult to earn and even tougher to keep. Critical thinking would tell us that for some people money is easy to earn and even easier to keep. For others, the opposite is true.

The point of dissecting critical thinking is not for the sake of semantics. It's to ground your thinking in objective reality as opposed to the half-fantasy, half-reality world in which most people live. Retiring rich requires seeing the world of money, saving and investing the way it really is as opposed to what the masses and the media want you to believe. Critical thinking tells us that millions of people, many of whom started saving and investing late in life, find a way to retire rich. Granted, it's a tiny percentage of people, but if they can do it, why can't you? We're not saying it will be simple or easy, but rather that it's possible. Any statements to the contrary are ignoring the facts. You can do this. Others have in the past and more will in the future. You have what it takes to become one of them.

> "Learn to use your brainpower. Critical thinking is the key to creative problem solving."
>
> *— Richard Branson*

CRITICAL THINKING QUESTION

In what areas of your life do you rely most on critical thinking?

ACTION STEP

List 3 areas of your retirement plan where you could employ less emotion and more critical thinking.

Chapter 25

Associate with Rich Retirees

Einstein said it best: consciousness is contagious. The people we associate with have an impact on our level of thinking. If you spend a lot of time with poor and middle-class retirees, you will likely end up with a fear and scarcity-based approach to your own retirement.

The key is to associate with rich retirees that are living their retirement dream. Unfortunately, these people are rare. According to a 2017 article published by Business Insider, the median value of assets for a 65-year-old married couple is $143,964. Now, the reality is that this money may have to last for 30 years, as people are living longer, healthier, more active lives. If you figure a 4% per year draw down for the average married couple with $143,964 net worth, we're talking about $5,758.56. This, combined with Social Security, doesn't add up to much.

Rich retirees are living a very different existence. You'll find them at country clubs, fundraisers, charity balls, and in towns like Palm Beach, Aspen and Beverly Hills. If you can't find a way to connect with them physically, associate with them through their books, social media, seminars, interviews and any other place in which they frequent. Watch their speeches and interviews online. The secret is to offset the negative programming and thinking of the masses with the positive, abundant thinking of the self-made rich. The exposure to their level of thinking and their fearless approach to life will inspire you to climb higher while expanding your expectations. Make a commitment to expose yourself to bigger thinkers on a daily basis and watch the impact it has on your consciousness. You'll begin to see the world through the eyes of the self-made rich, and the feelings it generates will give you hope for your future.

"You are who you associate with."

— *Tim Ferriss*

CRITICAL THINKING QUESTION

What is the approximate net worth of the people in which you spend the most time?

ACTION STEP

Attend one social event per quarter that gives you exposure to wealthier people.

Chapter 26

Listen to Your Heart/ Act with Your Head

For most people, money is an emotional subject. And if you want to retire rich, thinking this way is a mistake.

Life without emotion would be bland and boring. Emotion adds zest to our lives, and it has the power to motivate us to reach for the stars and achieve our dreams. The problem with emotion is that it clouds judgment and interferes in decision-making. In American society, money is among the most emotionally charged topics. If we have enough of it, it gives us security, sustenance and even luxury. In a capitalistic society, it's one of the ways we keep score and determine whether we are winning or losing. Many people define themselves by how much money they have, and others base their self-worth on their net worth. It determines where we live and how we live; where we work and what we do. Money is a big deal, and it's easy to allow our emotions to bleed over into our decision-making. When this happens we begin making decisions based on how they feel as opposed to what we think. It's the equivalent of making important financial decisions while intoxicated. The answer is to listen to your heart, but take action based on logical, evidenced-based critical thinking. This is a part of getting rich by getting tough.

Many financial moves feel good, but that doesn't mean you move forward based on that criteria alone. This is a common occurrence, but mostly among inexperienced investors or people looking for a quick buck. Think through every investment, and your money will grow safely. Employ logic with your money and emotion with your family, and never confuse the two.

"Individuals who cannot master their emotions are ill-suited to profit from the investment process."

— *Benjamin Graham*

CRITICAL THINKING QUESTION

As it relates to your retirement, are you listening to your heart and acting with your head?

ACTION STEP

Analyze the actions your taking towards your retirement and ask yourself if you're allowing emotion to misguide you.

Chapter 27

Study Taxation

If you want to retire rich, the government is not your friend.

There's an overwhelming ideology in Washington, D.C. that if you're rich, you should be punished for your success. They might not put you in jail, but they will tax you every way they can. That's why it's imperative that you study taxation and develop a working level of expertise. Most Americans have no idea that they are grossly overpaying on their taxes simply because they have never invested the time to study the tax code and laws. All of this information is available online, and with the new Trump tax overhaul in 2018, you need to know exactly where you stand. Like investment advisors, accountants can and do very widely in terms of their experience and expertise. Never cut corners when choosing an accountant or tax advisors. Cookie cutter tax experts often take the fastest path to completing your taxes, and that is never in your best interests. They don't do this out of malice or incompetence, but they're usually so overwhelmed with clients that they don't have time to do a thorough job on every return. I'm not suggesting you don't engage these experts. To the contrary, it's critical that you do. But just like investing, you must act as the Chief Operating Officer of your tax strategy. That means putting in the time to understand the most effective ways to minimize your taxes within the confines of the tax laws. There are many little known strategies that you can take advantage of, such as starting a business. The U.S. tax laws favor small business, and the money you can save just by hanging a shingle, is substantial. Most retirement vehicles are tax deferred, and your job is to protect every dollar you have from taxation so your money can grow through compound interest, minus the negative effect of eroding the principle through excessive taxation. So be sure to study taxation and stop paying more taxes then what is legally required.

> "The hardest thing to understand in the world is the income tax."
>
> *— Albert Einstein*

CRITICAL THINKING QUESTION

On a scale of 1-7, with 7 being most, how well do you understand the tax system?

ACTION STEP

Ask your advisor to explain the best tax strategies you can employ for retirement.

Chapter 28

Embrace Frugality

When you aspire to retire rich, the concept of frugality seemingly flies in the face of the abundance mindset required. Rich people usually come in one of three forms: the frugal miser who pinches pennies, the free-wheeling big spender, and the one that thinks big, lives large yet frugally, and carefully saves, invests, and watches over his money. Of these three, I'd recommend the latter.

You should adopt your own personal wealth philosophy, yet the choice seems clear: the frugal miser is rich in money, yet a pauper at heart. The free wheeling big spender is more of a show-off than a savvy investor. The big thinker that enjoys the fruits of his wealth yet watches over it carefully, is the guy that's figured it out. Some people believe thinking big and being frugal are mutually exclusive, but they're mistaken. Thinking big includes being smart, and being smart means there's a place for frugality in every rich person's life. In other words, when it's important that you invest in luxury, do it. And when the top of the line isn't important, be frugal and conserve your resources. The key is to make the distinction and follow the roadmap. It's based on an old self-made millionaire's axiom, which is: "You can have anything you want, just not everything you want at once." This philosophy keeps you thinking big, living large and acting smart.

> "Frugality is founded on the principle that all riches have limits."
>
> *— Edmund Burke*

CRITICAL THINKING QUESTION

How much money do you spend each month that you could be saving and investing?

ACTION STEP

Make a list of the areas of your life with which you can be more frugal, and another list of the areas where you can spend more in order to have the best quality of life.

Chapter 29

Stop Apologizing

Americans are brainwashed to believe that rich people are evil, shallow and selfish, and if you aspire to join them, you are a spiritually flawed human being. This is an ancient societal control strategy designed to keep the masses under the thumb of the government or ruling entity.

And it works. Ask 100 people on the street if they resent the rich, and 80% or more will answer affirmatively. It's no wonder, since this poverty-class programming continues through our college years. If you want to retire rich, you must reject this scarcity-based consciousness and adopt an attitude of abundance. It starts with a decision and solidifies with your refusal to apologize for seeking prosperity. Retiring rich is something of which to be proud. It's a badge of honor everyone would love to wear, yet most never will. The self-made rich have earned their money fairly in a free market economy. You don't get rich by chance or luck. Retiring rich comes as the result of years of sustained effort, painful failures and eventual breakthroughs. Accumulating wealth requires self-discipline and sacrifice. The last thing the rich retiree would consider is apologizing for his success. Any apology would negate years of blood, sweat and tears. Instead of apologizing for your success, stand up for the system that allowed you to achieve it and the people who mentored you along the way. Gratitude and humility go farther than false apologies.

Consider that if it were not for the ambitious, self-made man seeking his fortune, America would not have become the economic wonder of the world. America has never apologized for creating the highest standard of living in the history of the world, so why should you? Staking your claim has always been the American way, and retiring rich is staking your claim. Hold your head high for having the guts to go after the good life, and refuse to apologize to anyone when you arrive at your destination.

"Never apologize for your success. You worked for it."

— Goldie Hawn

CRITICAL THINKING QUESTION

Does the idea of retiring rich make you feel guilty?

ACTION STEP

Decide to stop apologizing for aspiring to retire rich. Instead, celebrate your ambition.

Chapter 30

Employ Emotional Motivators

Why do you want to retire rich? Besides securing a worry-free retirement, are there other factors driving you? Do you have something to prove? Do you see yourself living a lavish lifestyle? Would you prefer to enjoy your wealth in seclusion? The key to understanding the emotional motivators that govern our behavior is realizing that all benefits boil down to a feeling. In other words, it's not the beachfront home in Belize that's keeping me going, it's the feeling I imagine that I'll have when I'm living there. It's not the thought of drinking rum punch in Hawaii that gets my blood pumping, but how I believe I'll feel in the process of drinking it. In essence, it's not the money that motivates us, or even the things money will buy; it's the positive emotions we believe we'll experience.

This reflects the old adage that the most exciting part of purchasing your dream car is the day before you pick it up. Knowing what drives you emotionally gives you the power to pick yourself up and keep going long after everyone else has quit. Consider the idea that retiring rich means you won the game. This may not be politically correct, but it's true. According to a 2016 study of the Economic Policy Institute, only the top 1% of Americans had $1 million or more saved for retirement. And since a million isn't enough to retire rich, your self-made fortune places you among the richest people in the world. Few can lay claim to this badge of honor. Invest the time to identify your emotional motivators to sustain you through the tough times while propelling you even faster through the good times.

> "What's your why?"
>
> — *Eric Thomas*

CRITICAL THINKING QUESTION

What are you willing to fight for?

ACTION STEP

Make a list of your top five emotional motivators.

Chapter 31

Be Grateful

Bill Gove, the father of professional speaking, once said, "Gratitude is the aristocrat of all of the emotions." There is something about the mindset of gratitude that attracts people, opportunities and money. Is it the high frequency vibration that gratitude creates that acts as a magnet? Is it the relationships that are forged when grateful human beings connect on this elevated level of consciousness? Or possibly the expressed humility that's required to share gratitude? No one knows for sure, but what we do know is that gratitude is a mindset that manifests miracles – or at least, perceived miracles.

The only thing standing between you and a rich retirement is the help and support of enough other people. As simple as it sounds, it's true. Society has the power to make you rich. Your customers do, too. Even your competitors can make you rich. Living your life from a default mindset of gratitude is not only a world-class habit. It may also be the easiest and most effective relationship building strategy. It's easy to employ and build into your daily routine. Start out by writing a thank you note, email, text, or any other form of communication every morning before you start working. This simple, seemingly meaningless action will put you in the same energy vibration as the thoughts that inspired it. This will allow you to kick off each day in the right frame of mind, and move you closer to the success you seek. Try this strategy for 30 days and note the impact on your thinking. Not only will it put you in an attractive, high-level frequency, it will become the glue that makes your relationships last.

"Gratitude is the aristocrat of all of the emotions."

— *Bill Gove*

CRITICAL THINKING QUESTION

Would your closest friends and family consider you a grateful person?

ACTION STEP

Make a list of 10 things in your life for which you are most grateful.

Chapter 32

Forgive Yourself

Retiring rich, especially if you're starting late, requires the focus of a professional athlete, the concentration of a bullfighter and the mental toughness of a Navy SEAL. Earning, investing and saving money is the linear part of the equation. It's math. The hard part is the nonlinear aspect, which is the psychological, emotional side of being mentally prepared to do whatever it takes. Oddly enough, many experts agree that this is more of a subtraction process than an additive one. In other words, it's a matter of eliminating the thoughts, emotions and mental habits that cause interference and wreak havoc on our ability to sustain high performance.

One of the emotions that holds people back is the guilt they harbor for missed opportunities. Whether it's failing to invest early, losing money, not working harder, or any other guilt-ridden event, this emotion bogs us down and demotivates us. This is why it's imperative to your success that you learn to forgive yourself. Whatever your transgressions, you're not alone. All of us have made mistakes, and it's time to let them go.

If you want to retire rich, stop playing Atlas and let someone else carry the world. Haven't you held on to the guilt long enough? Guilt requires a tremendous amount mental energy that, once eliminated, can be redirected. Stop beating yourself up and start over. When it comes to the colossal goal of retiring rich, everyone deserves a second chance. Cut yourself some slack and free up your mind so you can finish strong.

> "The weak can never forgive. Forgiveness is the attribute of the strong."
>
> — *Mahatma Gandhi*

CRITICAL THINKING QUESTION

Have you forgiven yourself for the mistakes of your past?

ACTION STEP

Make a list of the major mistakes you've made in your life, forgive yourself for making them, and burn the list in your fireplace.

Chapter 33

Separate Logic and Emotion

Retiring rich requires years of logic-based critical thinking that leads to effective strategic planning. When it comes to saving and investing, the less emotion you inject into the process the more successful you will be. Emotion, like alcohol, impairs judgment, and it only takes a few poor judgment calls to eviscerate your retirement dream. Your best asset in growing your wealth is time, and mistakes can cost you a lot of it.

We all lived through the great recession, which started in 2008, and is now being referred to as 'the lost decade for investors'. If you were able to stay in the market and endure the downturn, you probably recouped your paper losses. On the other hand, if like the majority of Americans, you liquidated too early, you took a beating. You may have sold too soon out of necessity, or you may have allowed the emotion of fear to drive this decision. This is why it's critical that you compartmentalize your fear and base your financial decisions on logic.

Learning to compartmentalize your emotions is a world-class skill that's developed through practice. It's like a muscle: the more you use it, the stronger it gets. Practice keeping your emotions in check whenever you're discussing anything related to money, and you'll find yourself making fewer errors in judgment. Mental toughness, at its root, is essentially the ability to control and manipulate your emotions, especially under pressure. Everyone has this ability, but few master it. The secret is to practice anytime you are in an emotionally charged situation. Take note of how long you're able to control your emotions before they boil over. This applies to business conflicts, family situations and anything else where emotion begs to take over and render you stupid. Discipline yourself to avoid taking the emotional bait with which others are tempting you. Breathe, talk slowly and keep your voice down. No matter how wild your emotions are running on the inside, refuse to allow them to control your actions.

"If you don't control your emotions, your emotions will control your acts, and that's not good."

— *Marino Rivera*

CRITICAL THINKING QUESTION

On a scale of 1-7, with 7 being best, how well are you able to control your emotions?

ACTION STEP

Practice separating logic from emotion in everyday decision making.

Chapter 34

Invest in Your Interests

Successful investing is a tricky business. Some people believe in the passive approach of buy and hold, where you acquire an asset and forget about it. This serves a portion of the population, and this strategy has its advantages. Another approach is active investing, where you or someone you designate actively manages the investment. The active investing philosophy is to ensure that the asset is performing at its peak, and if something better comes along, to dump it and seek a better financial vehicle. Active investing is fun if you're interested in the asset in which you're investing, and if you're not interested in it, it's like watching paint dry.

Consider alternative investments as another way to grow your money, especially if you have a personal interest in the asset. For example, an alternative investment that has gained popularity in recent years is the vintage guitar market. This market is made up of guitar enthusiasts that love to acquire and sell old, valuable guitars. And some of them earn handsome profits. The secret to their success is that they love studying the vintage guitar market, and because they love it, they invest an inordinate amount of time in building an encyclopedic-like knowledge of the guitars and the market. These niche market investors evaluate these assets based on far greater criteria than the average mutual fund or equities investor. Collecting rare coins, cars, art, and lots of other areas where your favorite hobby could turn into your best investment.

Alternative, interest-based investing can be dangerous due to the emotional component. Falling in love with an investment can lead you to hold it longer than you should. That's the downside. The upside is it's fun when you can invest in something you love and earn a reasonable return. Be sure to consult a qualified expert in the specific alternative investment you're considering before moving forward.

....

"Do what you love and the money will follow."

— *Marsha Sinetar*

....

CRITICAL THINKING QUESTION

How much do you really know about your current investments?

ACTION STEP

Make a list of a few alternative investments in which you're interested and a105sk your advisor if any of them would fit into your retirement strategy.

Chapter 35

Don't Count on Luck

Retiring rich requires planning, effective strategy and hard work. There's a chance you may get lucky by timing the market, gaining access to (legal) inside information, or experience an unexpected windfall. All of these things are possible, yet improbable.

While this may sound like common sense, a large percentage of the population is betting their retirement on one of these events occurring. If it wasn't so dangerous, it might be funny – but the idea of being 85 years old and broke is anything but humorous. Millions of people head to Las Vegas and Atlantic City every year sincerely believing they are going to walk away wealthy. The same phenomenon occurs with the lottery. The people who play are middle-class or poor, and some experts believe the reason is hope. These people are struggling to stay afloat, and the small investment they make in a lottery ticket helps them keep that hope alive. In football, this would be called a "Hail Mary", which is a last-ditch effort to win the game with a spectacular play that has little chance of succeeding.

If you started saving and investing in your 40s, 50s or 60s, resist the urge to count on getting lucky to meet your retirement goals. Just because you're starting late doesn't mean you don't have time to make it. It's easier if you have more time, but that doesn't mean you can't pull it off. The right strategy and sound financial planning will give you a legitimate shot at the retirement life that you want to live.

And if you happen to get lucky in the process, take it. Just don't bet your savings on it.

> "I figure you have the same chance of winning the lottery whether you play or not."
>
> — *Fran Lebowitz*

CRITICAL THINKING QUESTION

Are you counting on luck to retire rich?

ACTION STEP

Make a commitment to abandon luck as a retirement strategy.

Chapter 36

Enjoy the Ride

Many people grow up being taught that money is not just the root of all evil, but a necessary evil. It's something that few like to discuss; yet everyone needs. And when it comes to saving for retirement, it's even less fun. We do the math, calculate the years we have remaining to fill our coffers with enough cash to live on until we die, and then hope for the best and plan for the worst. And for most of us, the math doesn't work during our early years, raising a family and staying afloat.

Once we get older and wiser, we realize that we have no choice. We must find a way to save and invest for the future, and then we put our heads down and go to work. In the process of building our retirement nest egg, many of us stress and struggle. We lay awake, lose sleep, and endure endless nights worrying that we won't have enough to retire. And even when we win, we still lose, because en route to reaching our retirement goal we suffered every step of the way. This is not the way to retire rich.

Decide now that you will enjoy the ride. The more you push yourself, the stronger you will grow and the more successful you will become. People who spend their days struggling attract more struggle; the same way that people who enjoy the process attract more enjoyment. If you think this is wishful thinking, consider the fact that some of the poorest countries in the world score the highest on the happiness index. This is possible because we all attract what we are, and if you're heart and mind are filled with love, joy and gratitude, you will attract more of each into your life. No matter how far away you are from your retirement dream, enjoy the ride, work hard to make it happen, and expect the best.

> "I've learnt that you never know what is around the corner, so it's best to enjoy the ride."
>
> — *Cush Jumbo*

CRITICAL THINKING QUESTION

Do you believe it's possible to enjoy the process of creating your rich retirement?

> **ACTION STEP**
>
> Identify three beliefs you would have to change in order to make your retirement journey more enjoyable.

Chapter 37

Upgrade Your Beliefs

One of the major distinctions between people who retire rich, and those who struggle, is what they believe about money, opportunity and wealth.

Many people are unaware of the power their belief system has in accumulating wealth, but our 34 year study of over 1,200 of the wealthiest people in the world shows that world-class beliefs almost always precede world-class wealth. The simple act of believing it's possible to retire rich will lead you to take the necessary actions to make it a reality. The belief that retiring rich is a positive goal worth pursuing leads to a mindset that prepares a person to make it happen. One of the most important beliefs you can adopt is that retiring rich means you are committed to creating extreme value for your customers and in return receiving abundant financial compensation. These world-class beliefs are held by a minority of population. The majority of people retire with minimal resources and tend to hold negative, disempowering beliefs around money. These beliefs relegate them to lower levels of success and prosperity. They buy into the mass consciousness that rich people are crooks and it's impossible for a rich man to go to heaven. These beliefs are brainwashed into most of us starting in early childhood, and by the time we're teenagers, we're programmed like robots to shun wealth and pursue economic mediocrity. Is it any wonder so few of us retire rich?

No matter what your current beliefs are about money, the key is to upgrade them immediately. Study what rich people think about money and then copy their beliefs. You re-program your mind the same way you were programmed in the first place: through time and repetition. Except this time, you'll develop beliefs that will serve you instead of keeping you poor.

"Believe you can and you're halfway there."

— *Theodore Roosevelt*

CRITICAL THINKING QUESTION

What core beliefs do you have that threaten your future prosperity?

ACTION STEP

Take your 5 most limiting beliefs around money and upgrade them to serve your best interests.

Chapter 38

Think Like a Comeback Artist

If you're among the small percentage of people who have been preparing for your retirement since your first paycheck, congratulations. On the other hand, if you started saving and investing later in life and you find yourself behind the proverbial eight ball, this strategy will serve you well. Instead of thinking that you're behind, begin seeing yourself as a comeback artist.

In professional sports, the comeback artist ranks high on the list of dangerous competitors. You can never count these people out, because they never count themselves out. They're able to perform at consistently high levels, whether they're winning or losing. It's as though they don't understand they are losing, and before you know it, they're able to turn things around and take the trophy. It's more of a mindset than a talent, and while some people appear to be born with it, most learn it through necessity. The outlook of the comeback artist is positive, proactive, and most of all, persistent. Persistent to the point where most rational thinkers would count them out with a condescending smile, right before they take the lead and retire rich. The comeback artist may not always win, but he always thinks he's going to win, which is all the psychological fuel he needs to keep moving forward, against all odds.

If you're behind in your effort to retire rich, make a decision to adopt the comeback artist mentality, and never say die. No matter if you're 40, 50, 60, or 70, anyone that embraces this mentality can never be counted out. A comeback artist always has a chance. As long as you're living and breathing, keep pushing forward with persistence and mental toughness until you either retire rich or die trying. That's the mantra of the professional comeback artist.

"I've missed more than 9,000 shots in my career. I've lost almost 300 games. 26 times, I've been trusted to take the game winning shot and missed. I've failed over and over and over again in my life. And that is why I succeed."

— *Michael Jordan*

CRITICAL THINKING QUESTION

When it comes to your retirement, do you see yourself as comeback artist?

ACTION STEP

Start telling yourself that you are a comeback artist, and that you're proving it every day that you move closer to retiring rich.

Chapter 39

Control Your Fear

Fear is a default defense mechanism. It serves us well, and according to scientists, has helped our species survive for at least 100,000 years. The problem is that once we are safe and secure, fear limits our success. And when it comes to retiring rich, the last thing we need is limitation.

This is why it's imperative that we face our fears. Psychologists say that confronting our fears is the fastest way to reduce their significance. It's like standing up to the bully in school. It's scary, yet once you do it, the fear begins to diminish. Begin to confront your biggest retirement fears, starting with not having enough money to live until you die. How about fears that relate to your family? Are you worried that you'll die and leave your family with bills they can't pay? These are just a few of the most common fears we hear from people planning for retirement, and they are valid. As a matter of fact, most major fears in life are justifiable. The problem is they're not helpful. The fear of coming up short in retirement may drive you to aggressive action and Zen-like fiscal discipline, but too much fear can paralyze you. Fear leads to apathy and the feeling that retiring rich is merely a pipe dream. It's not, and most of your success depends on you. This begins by mentally feeding your vision of an exciting, abundant retirement, while simultaneously starving your deepest fears.

Control your fear by inundating your mind with thoughts, feelings and mental images of a limitless retirement.

Instead of avoiding your fears, invest so much time envisioning your ideal future that there's little space or time for anything else.

> "Do what you fear most, and you control fear."
>
> *— Tom Hopkins*

CRITICAL THINKING QUESTION

Do you operate from a mindset of fear and scarcity or love and abundance?

ACTION STEP

Identify your 3 biggest fears about retiring rich and the worst things that can happen if they are realized.

Chapter 40

Sleep with One Eye Open

Watch your money, always. Not just the dollars, but also the quarters, dimes, nickels and pennies. When you're attempting a goal as large as retiring rich, every penny counts. Always sleep with one eye open.

Now while this sounds like a fear-driven philosophy, it's simply a prudent strategy. As the old adage goes: trust, but verify. This is especially important when empowering someone to manage your money, recommend investments or engage in any activity that places your money at risk. There are a lot of good, hard-working, honest people in the money business. And there are also a lot of self-serving brokers who legally do not have to act in your best interests. This doesn't only apply to the financial services industry, but to every industry where collusion and inherent conflicts of interest are potentially profitable. Easy money has a strong appeal, and people who are naturally honest can begin to blur the lines between what's good for their client and what's good for them.

Don't allow this to stop you from working with partners, advisors who, by law, are legally required to act in your best interests and others who can help you, just be sure that you know as much about the investments they're recommending as they do. Never rush into a financial instrument or contract because you're being pressured to meet some imaginary deadline. Usually that's only a commission deadline for the broker or salesperson. Invest as much time as possible to study, dissect, and conduct due diligence. This strategy will ensure that you'll move forward on investments that you understand and believe in, and it will also help you sleep better at night. The more you understand about your investments, the closer you will be to your money.

> "Do your homework so you can listen to the answers and react to them and ask follow-ups. Do your homework, prepare."
>
> — *Jim Lehrer*

CRITICAL THINKING QUESTION

On a scale of 1-7, with 7 being most, how closely are you watching over your retirement money?

ACTION STEP

Wherever you rated yourself on the 1-7 scale, make a commitment to always be a 7.

Chapter 41

Embrace the Suck of Investing

The financial rewards of investing are reserved for the future, which is one of the reasons so few people are willing to commit to it. It's more fun to spend money now than it is to save for the future. Buying feels good, and many of us are emotionally addicted to the feeling we experience when we acquire something we desire. Investing for the future doesn't give us the emotional high that we crave as consumers.

This is why you must embrace the suck of investing by imagining how you're going to feel when you retire rich. In times past, pension programs created forced retirement savings where money was being banked every pay period to help fund every employee's retirement. Well, as you know, those days are gone. Today your savings program is up to you, and as expected, most people are opting out. The secret of retiring rich is disciplining yourself to invest whatever you can, as often as you can, as early in life as you can. Invest a percentage of your paycheck every payday and try to increase that percentage every year.

It's probably not going to be fun. No more than going to the dentist. Not every activity in life is enjoyable, but some are necessary for survival. And make no mistake: preparing for retirement is a matter of survival. Yes, you're young, strong and energetic. And hopefully you will thrive in this state for many years. But someday your body will break down, your strength will weaken and your energy will flatten.

It's tough, but that's life. The key is to embrace it and prepare so you can retire rich and pay for whatever help you need. Money won't make you younger, but it will make being older infinitely easier.

> "Patience, persistence and perspiration make an unbeatable combination for success."
>
> — *Napoleon Hill*

CRITICAL THINKING QUESTION

How do you think you'll feel when you retire rich?

ACTION STEP

List the 5 most positive emotions you will experience when you retire rich.

Chapter 42

Brush off the Losses

Investing can be risky, especially if you're young and chasing big returns. Aggressive investing is not for the faint of heart, but it can be rewarding. Ask anyone whose doubled his money in the market. Each investor must decide on the level of risk they wish to take. It's a subjective decision based on multiple criteria and is best determined with the assistance of a trusted fiduciary advisor.

Even with moderately aggressive investments, it's easy to lose money. Every investor has at least one story of betting on the wrong horse and coming up short. No matter what level of risk you decide to take, when you lose, the secret is to brush it off. Don't waste time and energy berating yourself, because the truth is, you're in good company. Even the titans of Wall Street lose. It's just part of the game. Money is important, but it's not worth destroying your peace of mind. As the old saying goes, you place your bets and you take your chances, and then you let the chips fall where they may. If you win, be happy and recognize that there may have been some good fortune involved. Sometimes you're at the right place at the right time. And if you lose, be happy that you didn't lose more. Be happy that you had the money to lose, learn from it and move on.

Never allow yourself to wallow in the self-pity of your losses. It's not only a waste of time; it's a waste of energy that's better directed toward your next investment. Whether you're making a killing or losing a fortune, make a decision to be your own best friend.

> "Every day is a new day, and you'll never be able to find happiness if you don't move on."
>
> — *Carrie Underwood*

CRITICAL THINKING QUESTION

How much psychological/emotional baggage are you carrying around from previous financial losses?

ACTION STEP

Make a decision to forgive yourself for all of your past financial mistakes.

Chapter 43

Call on Your Courage

It takes courage to set a goal to retire rich. Of course, rich is a relative term, and you have to determine what it means to you and how much you'll have to accumulate to achieve it. Regardless of the amount, you'll need courage to make it happen. Every time you make a long-term investment, you are betting on yourself to be able to sustain your lifestyle in the near term.

Growing money tax deferred for retirement means it's no longer liquid, and if for some reason you're forced to withdraw it, you'll pay a stiff penalty that will likely erase previous gains. Spending is easy. Banking cash is easy. Investing your hard earned money in financial vehicles where you won't see your money for years, possibly even decades, takes courage.

Retiring rich is as much of a mental game as it is a financial game, and the core of the game is courage. It's no different than putting yourself on a diet. It's a simple process, but you're suddenly limited to what and when you can eat. And when you've spent your entire life eating anything and everything, it's a major shift in thinking. The shorter the retirement window, the more courage will be required to spend less and save more. It's always tempting to spend now and invest later, but as the months turn into years, and the years into decades, you wake up one day and realize that it's never an easy time. Call on your courage to do what it takes to win the game. When you no longer have the energy and vitality to compete, you'll be glad you did.

> "Success is not final, failure is not fatal: it is the courage to continue that counts."
>
> — *Winston Churchill*

CRITICAL THINKING QUESTION

Do you believe you have the courage to do what it takes to retire rich?

ACTION STEP

Decide what you will have to do to gather the courage to retire rich.

Chapter 44

Stay Excited

When most of us think about investing for retirement, the word 'enthusiasm' usually does not come to mind. To most of us, building a retirement portfolio is a boring, banal, necessary evil. But the truth is it doesn't have to be.

The idea of spending your golden years free of financial concerns is exciting, but only if you believe you have a legitimate shot. The lack of belief is one of the primary reasons people fail to save and invest. They look at their salary, tally their bills and wonder how they're going to survive today much less retire rich tomorrow. The fact is that it's not an easy thing to do. If it were, everyone would be retiring to the south of France and traveling the world on their yacht.

In our research, one of the key strategies practiced by successful people is maintaining their level of excitement as they pursue their goals and dreams. It's easy to be excited when you're portfolio is bursting with big returns, but the secret is staying excited when you're years behind schedule. Getting excited about your eventual success is a skill you acquire through persistence and practice. If you don't feel excited, we recommend that you fake it until you feel it. It's the purposeful manipulation of your emotions, and it works. Staying excited about your bountiful future and the process of building it should be your ultimate goal.

You see; retiring rich is more than a financial destination. It's a self-affirming psychological journey you will be proud that you traveled for the rest of your life. Only a small percentage of people retire with millions of dollars, and imagine the pride you'll feel as you move closer to becoming one of them.

"Nothing great was ever achieved without enthusiasm."

— *Ralph Waldo Emerson*

CRITICAL THINKING QUESTION

When it comes to your retirement, would you consider yourself enthusiastic?

ACTION STEP

Identify one action you can take to increase your enthusiasm.

Chapter 45

Build Psychological Momentum

As emotion-driven creatures, human beings thrive on momentum. The hardest part of building momentum is in the beginning; where you have to push the hardest to get things moving forward. When it comes to building momentum for retirement, the biggest step in the process is the first.

Looking down the road 10, 20, or 30 years at your retirement and calculating the amount of money you need for a 30 year run can be daunting at best and paralyzing at worst. This is especially true if you're starting with little or no savings. Maybe you've been putting your kids through college, or investing in your business and haven't allocated the funds towards retirement. Now you're looking up the steep side of a mountain that you must climb in a relatively ridiculous period of time, and it seems hopeless. It's not. Even if you have 10 years to amass your fortune, you have to believe that it's not only possible, but also probable.

The secret is to start now and begin building psychological momentum. That means putting something away today, not tomorrow, and observe how it makes you feel. I guarantee it will make you feel good. And then tomorrow, we want you to do the same thing. We don't care if you're investing a lot or a little, the key is to invest something, anything; that will start the flow of psychological momentum. Gather the loose change in your car and put it in the bank. Clean out the attic and sell some old things on EBay that are gathering dust. Drive a couple of hours a week for Uber or Lyft and put the profits in a savings account. As small as these actions seem, they serve as building blocks of momentum that will lead to larger opportunities and bigger deposits. If you'll have the courage to take the first step, you'll be surprised at how good it will make you feel.

> "One way to keep momentum going is to have constantly greater goals."
>
> *— Michael Korda*

CRITICAL THINKING QUESTION

On a scale of 1-7, with 7 being most, how would you rate your retirement momentum?

ACTION STEP

Take one action every week to increase your retirement momentum, such as saving money you would normally spend or working extra hours to increase your income.

Chapter 46

Just Say No

Retiring rich means learning how to say no to yourself and others when it comes to anything that threatens your long-term goal. This includes saying no to needless spending, vacations, cars, homes, and even time off.

Succeeding will require changing the way you run your life, allocate your time, and choose your friends. If you're socializing with people who don't support your goals, you may need to curtail these activities. When they ask you to do things that are incongruent with where you're going, you'll have to say no. Bowling on Wednesday night might be fun, but working overtime would move you closer to your goal. Having drinks on the town might be entertaining, but saving that money by hanging at home would be more prudent. This is part of the price for retiring rich.

While these examples are obvious, don't expect your friends to understand. People don't like being denied, and it may create friction in your relationships. But when you're ready to retire, these people won't be offering to pay your bills. Statistics show that the majority of them will be struggling in old age to sustain their lifestyle. Being elderly is tough enough without adding financial struggles to the mix. The way to get good at saying no is to start now. This will save you time, money and aggravation, but it may cost you relationships. That's the downside of serving your own best interests. Most people would rather focus on today and forget about tomorrow. It's a foolish strategy practiced by the masses. Break out of their losing philosophy by saying no early and often, and not being offended or upset by the backlash it may create.

> "The key is not to prioritize what's on your schedule, but to schedule your priorities."
>
> — *Stephen Covey*

CRITICAL THINKING QUESTION

How comfortable are you with saying no?

> **ACTION STEP**
>
> Make a decision to start saying no to anything that threatens your retirement goals.

Chapter 47

Seek Solitude

Successful investing requires clear, concise, critical thinking over a long period of time. Markets go up and down, jobs come and go, and businesses experience highs and lows. This is why it's essential that you become mentally tough as you build your fortune. Without the grit to hang tough over an extended period of time, you will not be able to endure the challenges.

One of the primary causes of psychological/emotional breakdown is excessive cognition. In other words, the experience of being overrun with thoughts, worries and problems. It's similar to when you have too many files open on your computer. First the speed of the computer slows down, and if you continue opening new windows, it will eventually crash. The same thing happens in the human brain. When too many thoughts are dominating our minds, our processing ability begins to slow. This is a common occurrence in corporate America, although it's not well understood and rarely addressed.

One of the secrets to avoiding excessive cognition is to create more space between your thoughts by seeking solitude. Find a place you can go to escape the barrage of information you're hit with on a daily basis. If you can't get away, use meditation to move your mind to a peaceful place. This will give your mind the rest it needs to perform at its best.

Create a daily habit of seeking solitude in one form or another, and you'll think more clearly and better endure the stressors of daily life. A rested mind will help you make better investments, not to mention that it will make the process of building your retirement portfolio more peaceful and enjoyable.

> "Solitude is creativity's best friend, and solitude is refreshment for our souls."
>
> — *Naomi Judd*

CRITICAL THINKING QUESTION

How much solitude do you get during the course of an average week?

ACTION STEP

Commit to getting at least 1 hour of solitude per week.

Chapter 48

Visualize Your Retirement

Once you decide on the details of your retirement, it's time to create a mind movie visualization to turn your words into pictures. Rehearsing these images in your mind has multiple benefits.

One benefit is the systematic, psychological imprinting that visualization accomplishes. Seeing yourself sitting on a beach in Costa Rica, sipping a fruity drink with an umbrella on top brings out the emotion you believe you will experience. The pictures create clarity, but it's the emotional charge that the pictures create that is the real power behind visualization. And the more you practice, the clearer the pictures become and the stronger the emotion grows.

Another benefit is getting to experience how it feels to live your fantasy retirement. It's like test-driving your retirement to see if it's what you truly desire. Sometimes lazy days of lying on the beach or traveling around the world are better in fantasy. Many people who look forward to retirement wind up bored and unsatisfied. Visualizing will help reduce the chance of this happening to you.

You may discover during your visualizations that you need more money to do what you really want to do, and this gives you time to build it into your plan. Maybe you're planning on retiring at 65, but after visualizing a beach house that costs more money, you decide to bump it up until 70. You may go the opposite way and find that you don't need as fancy a lifestyle as you had originally thought, and this means you won't need as much money. Visualization offers the opportunity to see your future in advance, as well as the opportunity to change it whenever you choose.

"Visualize this thing that you want, see it, feel it, believe in it. Make your mental blue print, and begin to build."

— *Robert Collier*

CRITICAL THINKING QUESTION

How often have you used visualization in the past?

ACTION STEP

Begin visualizing your rich retirement for 5 minutes per day.

Chapter 49

Embrace Cause and Effect

To keep your thinking grounded in objective reality, consider the impact of cause and effect. This is one of the most effective psychological strategies you can employ. The main thing to remember is that every cause has an effect, including every action you take, or don't take, towards your retirement goals. Even the smallest, seemingly meaningless act, creates an effect. In essence, everything counts, because everything you do affects everything else.

On the surface, the concept of cause and effect seems simple, but in actuality, it's not. Investing 1% of your weekly paycheck would appear to be a small action, but the corresponding effects include not only your retirement account, but also how you feel about it and the emotional momentum it can create. Some experts have labeled this the 'ripple effect,' in reference to tossing a pebble into a pond and watching the ripples reverberate beyond its point of entry. It's a powerful metaphor, yet due to its physical specificity, it's limited to a physical effect.

The point of this is to recognize that everything you do creates a series of effects that often go far beyond your intentions. This is why it's critical that you become acutely aware of every action you take towards retirement. Carefully consider the consequences, including those that are unintended, of every move you make. Positive actions, like studying money, consistent investing, following trusted advisors are all causes with corresponding effects. Negative actions work the same way, and their effects can be detrimental to your goals. Begin paying attention to what happens as a result of your saving and investment decisions, including physically, mentally, emotionally and spiritually. Recognizing these effects will lead you towards overwhelmingly positive actions, while avoiding sloppy, negative actions that threaten to derail your retirement dreams.

"The complexities of cause and effect defy analysis."

— *Douglas Adams*

CRITICAL THINKING QUESTION

Are your actions towards retirement creating the effects for which you're looking?

ACTION STEP

Make a list of the 5 most important actions you're taking towards retiring rich.

Chapter 50

Study Markets

Getting tough so you can retire rich is more than just building emotional strength and resiliency. It's about becoming self-reliant when it comes to growing your portfolio. This means investing time to study specific markets in which you are interested in investing.

One of the keys to successful investing is education. Modern technology has made it possible to learn from world-class experts, for free, on websites like YouTube and others. The more you can learn, the more successful you will be and the better you will sleep at night. Whether it's learning how to find hidden fees in mutual funds or developing expertise in renting residential real estate, a commitment to ongoing study will pay off handsomely.

While we advocate paying for advice from independent advisors, there's no way to overstate the difference it makes to know what questions to ask while having the ability to know if you're getting accurate answers. Retiring rich means taking on responsibility for your own financial success, no matter how many outside experts are guiding you. This study requires daily discipline, but few activities will pay off more handsomely. To build your study into a daily habit, begin by dedicating 10 minutes a day towards this activity. Select an investment area that you're interested in, and study it for 10 minutes a day. Take notes at every session and write down follow up questions. And if you find yourself bored in the process, choose a different investment.

There are lots of different ways to invest your money, so study one that appeals to you. You'll be surprised at how quickly you will develop a working knowledge of the investment you choose. The more you learn, the more you will enjoy the process.

> "Education is the most powerful weapon which you can use to change the world."
>
> — *Nelson Mandela*

CRITICAL THINKING QUESTION

How much do you know about money and markets?

ACTION STEP

Commit to 10 minutes of daily study of money and markets.

Chapter 51

Compartmentalize Your Emotions

Money and emotion make bad bedfellows. They just don't mix. The old, yet simple axiom, tells us not to get emotional about money. This seems easy enough, right up to the point where you fall in love with the investment or the promise of outstanding returns. That's when emotional drunkenness takes over and logic goes out the door.

The two most dangerous emotions for investors are fear and greed, which are the same two emotions that drive markets to overvaluation and cause economies to recede. When the market is hot, everyone wants in. When the markets are cold, everyone wants out. And since markets are in a constant cycle of hot and cold, either fear or greed is in play at all times. This is not for you.

The key to avoiding this emotional rollercoaster is learning to compartmentalize your emotions. In other words, keeping your emotions in a psychological compartment that's opened only when it serves your best interests. This is a skill all of us use on a regular basis, although few are probably conscious of it. We know as mature adults that the anger and frustration we feel after a morning fight with our spouse cannot be carried into the workplace. We've learned how to store our emotions away so we can do what we need to do without emotional interference.

This skill works well when evaluating spending, investing and saving decisions because it calls on your logic-based critical thinking without emotion clouding your judgment. The more you practice compartmentalizing, the better you'll get. Use this strategy with every financial decision.

> "In the world of money and investing, you must learn to control your emotions."
>
> — *Robert Kiyosaki*

CRITICAL THINKING QUESTION

How have you used compartmentalization in the past to serve your best interests?

ACTION STEP

Practice concentrating on one thing at a time and see how long you can focus before thinking of something else. The more you practice the longer you will be able to focus on a single subject.

Chapter 52

Expect a Fight

A lot of people we've consulted with over the years have fallen under the false expectation that retiring rich was going to be easy. Most of these people had six and seven-figure incomes, and because of that, they assumed that no matter how much money they spent, they would always have additional funds to invest in retirement. Despite years of pleading with them to curb spending and start investing, many continued to falsely believe that their high income would translate into high net worth. Another issue we've seen with clients is the belief that somehow, when they got older, they were going to be the recipient of a financial windfall that would fund their retirement. For most, this was a simple case of wishful thinking, and for others, it was outright delusion.

For most of us, retiring rich is not going to be easy. That's why it's critical that you expect to fight for it. I'm not talking about fighting against other people. This is an internal battle. It's you against you. It's your adolescent self versus your adult self. It's your ego versus your spirit. It's the best of you versus the worst of you. It's one thing to retire modestly, and quite another to retire rich. Anyone can downsize their lifestyle, sell off possessions and frugally live out their retirement years. That's exactly what most Americans do. There's nothing wrong with that. You don't need a book to teach you how to do that. This book is about retiring rich. It's about going full throttle and refusing to settle for less.

So don't be surprised when you are frustrated, angry and impatient along this journey. To the contrary, you should expect to experience all of these emotions and more. It's just part of the fight. Embrace it, accept it, and keep moving forward like the winner you are.

"Nothing that comes easy is worth a dime."

— *Woody Hayes*

CRITICAL THINKING QUESTION

How much are you willing to suffer so you can retire rich?

ACTION STEP

List the top 5 sacrifices you will have to make to retire rich.

Chapter 53

Stop Keeping Up with the Joneses

One of the biggest mistakes you can make is allowing your ego to purchase overpriced, non-income producing assets for the purpose of impressing your friends.

This is so prevalent in middle-class America that we have a phrase that describes it as 'keeping up with the Joneses.' This phrase is a common part of our vernacular because so many of us fall for this insidious trap. Let's call a spade a spade: flashy possessions make us feel important. They give us a level of satisfaction and show others how successful and important we are. The one tenth of one percent of money earners do more of this than anyone. They fly in private planes, live on multiple continents and vacation on their own islands. They can afford it. And if you're in that category, earning at least $9.5 million dollars per year, you have our permission to skip this chapter.

But if you're like the majority of mere mortals earning less, this is an important lesson to consider. Impressing people with possessions is expensive, and it threatens to eat away at the financial reserves you need to invest in assets that can grow tax deferred for decades. So are we suggesting that you drive an old beat up car and live in a trailer? No. When you're doing well financially, you can afford to live well, and you can even purchase flashy possessions. You just can't purchase them all. This is how professional football and basketball players blow hundred-million-dollar fortunes. It's easy to spend money, and it's fun. You just have to do it in moderation and make sure that your retirement investments are tracking with your goals. Besides, no one cares about your new Ferrari. Your success has no meaning to anyone outside of you and your family.

> "The ultimate aim of the ego is not to see something, but to be something."
>
> — *Muhammad Iqbal*

CRITICAL THINKING QUESTION

How much money have you spent in the past for the purpose of keeping up with the Joneses?

ACTION STEP

When it comes to buying things to impress people, make a decision to abandon your ego and start on the new journey of investing your money only to serve your best interests.

Chapter 54

Be Doggedly Persistent

When it comes to saving and investing, nothing can replace the power of persistence. You can be the most highly intelligent, Ivy League educated person on the planet, but if you don't persist in the face of failure, you're going to be working a lot longer than you probably want to. Investing and growing a seven-figure portfolio is not a linear process. Markets go up and down. Some investments are winners, and others, losers. Sometimes long shots pay off, and other times they don't. Retiring rich is not a sprint; it's a marathon. And it's a marathon filled with fun, excitement, frustration, disappointment and just about every other emotional up and down you can imagine. If retiring rich were easy, everyone would have millions of dollars in the bank on their last day of work. They don't.

The research shows that only 3.5% of retirees have at least one million dollars in retirement savings. That's not surprising. What is surprising is the reason they have so little money, which is their lack of persistence in investing early and sticking to it without deviation. Persistence is easy when the market is up and you're flying high, but the mentally tough investor persists no matter what's happening in the markets. In sports, this is how a quarterback whose team is down by 25 points in the Super Bowl comes back and wins. It's how a Navy SEAL team trains for 10 years for a single opportunity to bring a terrorist to justice. It's how a parent works and struggles for 18 years to raise a child through thick and thin to prepare him to face the world.

Persistence is to retiring rich what carbon is to steel. It's the foundation. Persistence isn't always pretty, yet it continues moving forward undeterred by obstacles, failures and frustrations to eventually reach its ultimate destiny.

"Paralyze resistance with persistence."

— *Woody Hayes*

CRITICAL THINKING QUESTION

How would your best friend rate your overall level of persistence?

ACTION STEP

Start telling yourself that you are the most persistent person in the world.

Chapter 55

Control Your Ego

Along with controlling your emotions comes controlling your ego. When it comes to retiring rich, there's no place for pride. It's a process that continues for years, and oftentimes, it's not pretty. You don't hit a home run every time, and sometimes you strike out.

The psychological approach you want to take is cool, calm and collected. Steady as she goes. You don't want to get too hyped up about the gains, and not too worried about the losses. It's a long haul, and pacing yourself emotionally is key. When you're winning, it's easy to let your ego run wild. If we had a nickel for every country club party we've attended where guys with monster egos were bragging over booze about how they timed the market, we'd be a lot richer. These braggarts love to espouse their brilliant investment theories, and the more booze goes down, the bigger the story grows. You'll notice that there's never any mention of losses, because apparently, these people never lose. Warren Buffet makes a bad call now and then and discusses it on CNBC, but these guys make money with every risk they take.

Don't believe it for a second, and more importantly, don't fall into the trap of buying into the idea that you're going to beat the market. Investment markets can be as friendly as a puppy and as dangerous as a rattlesnake. Yes, if you do your homework, heed good advice from experts, and take modest, calculated risks, you can retire rich. But if you get a few wins and get cocky, the market will hand you your head. And you won't be the first. Even the best and brightest on Wall Street get humbled from time to time. So stay grounded and focused, and only associate with other investors who do the same.

> "The ego is nothing other than the focus of conscious attention."
>
> — *Alan Watts*

CRITICAL THINKING QUESTION

On a scale of 1-7, with 7 being biggest, how would you rate your ego?

ACTION STEP

Make a commitment to reduce the size of your ego and begin operating from more of a spirit-based consciousness.

Chapter 56

Embrace Boring Investments

Some of the best investments you can make are also some of the most boring. Monitoring their turtle-speed growth is as exciting as watching paint dry. Train your mind to focus on slow, steady gradual growth. Sexy stocks, start-ups and mind blowing new technology may be exciting, but they are also loaded with risk that may threaten your progress. This is more of a mental discipline than a fiscal strategy, which is why you should think clearly and move slowly when presented with the next flashy investment.

An example of this are Marijuana stocks*, which are all the rage right now. Millions of excited investors are pouring into penny stocks and blue chips alike, attempting to cash in on this so-called 21st century gold rush. People are cashing in their 401k's, mortgaging their homes and raiding their kid's college funds in hopes of striking it rich. Without a crystal ball, it's impossible to know whether or not this is a good idea. Maybe investing in these stocks will turn out to be a wise choice, or maybe these companies will fold. The point is that the sexier the stock, the easier it is to persuade people to buy it, and the more likely you are to get sucked into a bad investment.

If you have money to burn, you may elect to gamble on flashy investments. Just beware that these plays can be double-edged swords, and they can eat money as fast as you can feed it. For safety reasons, embrace the boring and leave the high risk plays to the professional gamblers on Wall Street.

*Steve Siebold holds several positions in Marijuana equities.

> "Rule No.1: Never lose money. Rule No.2: Never forget rule No.1."
>
> *— Warren Buffett*

CRITICAL THINKING QUESTION

Do you gravitate towards flashy investments?

ACTION STEP

Restrain yourself from basing your investment decisions on outward appearances.

Chapter 57

Build or Buy a Business

Another smart strategy is starting your own business. The right product or service delivered at the right time is one of the best ways to bolster your portfolio. If you have the expertise, discipline and desire to work long hours for little pay, buying or building a business might be right for you. And if you're content with sticking with your current job or career, you might consider partnering with someone who would run the day-to-day operations in partnership with your financing.

Now, buyer-beware: if you've never owned a business, make sure you enter this arena with your eyes wide open. Operating a small business, or even financing one, is not for the faint of heart. The potential is tremendous, but the work and worry can be overwhelming. New businesses eat cash, and there are never any guarantees that you'll get it back. Making payroll, purchasing inventory, paying taxes and acquiring customers can take a toll on both body and mind. Every entrepreneur knows what it's like to be staring at the ceiling at 3am, wondering how you're going to open the doors in the morning with no money to meet payroll. It's a burden that never goes away.

That being said, once you're up and running, the profits can be substantial. Depending on the business, you can sock away more money in a year than most people do in a lifetime. The heart of starting and operating a successful business is passion, because before the money starts rolling in, that's all you have to show for it. If your time horizon for retirement is short, this may be your best chance to catch up. Few investments can match the profit potential of a successful small business. Be sure to perform your due diligence before starting any business. The more aware you are of the risks and pitfalls, the better chance you will have to succeed.

> "I believe that starting any business should be as easy as a 10-year-old starting a lemonade stand."
>
> — *Mark Cuban*

CRITICAL THINKING QUESTION

If you were to start a business, what would it be?

ACTION STEP

Identify several businesses you could afford to start and operate.

Chapter 58

Stop Tolerating Mediocrity

Retiring rich is a process that starts and ends with you. It's a financial and mental game rolled into one. The financial strategies are important, but the mental aspects will determine whether you win or lose.

One of the first steps is to stop tolerating mediocrity in your life, especially with yourself. None of us are perfect, but we are all capable of demanding more from ourselves. The mindset embraced by the masses only yields mediocre results, and that's why it's necessary to upgrade your mental game and adopt world-class philosophies.

Start by eating less and exercising more. Improve your diet. If you're overweight, lose it. Drink less alcohol and more water. If you smoke, reduce the number or quit. Sleep seven or eight hours per night. Be in bed by 10 and up by 6. Resolve relationship problems with people you love and be at peace with yourself. Turn off the TV and start reading. Be present during family time and date night. Listen twice as much as you talk. Get a physical examination and dental cleaning. Forgive yourself and others. Smell the roses. Meditate. Breathe. Relax. And the list goes on.

You already know these things, but how many are you doing? The tougher you are on yourself, the easier it will be to win. Good habits produce positive results. It's hard to stop a man who pushes himself to strive for excellence, both physically and mentally. It's easy to follow the masses, but it won't produce a world-class life. Promise yourself that starting today; you will begin holding yourself to a higher standard: a standard that is worthy of who you are. A standard that represents your ambition, education and mental toughness. A standard that you deserve. And then sit back and watch how your new world begins to unfold.

"Set your goals high, and don't stop till you get there."

— *Bo Jackson*

CRITICAL THINKING QUESTION

In what areas of your life have you tolerated mediocrity?

ACTION STEP

Decide today not to accept a mediocre retirement.

Chapter 59

Monitor Your Thinking and Language

Building a modest net worth is a linear process. Amassing a world-class net worth is more of a non-linear, psychological process. Your decisions surrounding everything financial will be based on your beliefs, tolerance for risk and ability to control and sustain your emotions.

Most people don't believe this. They believe that acquiring money is simply a matter of math. If that were actually true, every financial planner, banker and math teacher would be rich. But they're not, and most of them never will be. Retiring rich doesn't mean you have superior math skills or even a better financial planner. The heart of most self-made fortunes is the level of thinking that created it. This is why you must monitor your thoughts, and make a habit out of rejecting fear-based, scarcity thinking. Become acutely aware of your environment, both physical and mental. Move yourself out of any emotional climate that is not conducive to a higher level of consciousness. In addition, do the same with the language you use with other people and yourself. As the old cliché goes, we become what we think about, most of the time.

If you want to retire rich, you have to think like someone who already has. People with an excess of money tend to be calm, cool and collected when it comes to earning, saving and investing. They spend most of their time in what psychologists call 'emotional neutral.' This helps establish the proper mental climate for peak performance and rich thinking to occur.

Start to notice how many of your daily thoughts are rooted in love and abundance versus fear and scarcity. Next, begin shifting your fear-based thoughts to love and abundance, and you'll be on your way. You'll be surprised at how fast this action will become a habit.

"Your positive action combined with
positive thinking results in success."

— *Shiv Khera*

CRITICAL THINKING QUESTION

Is your self-talk more middle class or world class?

ACTION STEP

Begin monitoring everything you say to yourself and others and upgrade any limiting language

RECOMMENDED RESOURCE

The Making of a Million Dollar Mind (Audio series)
www.milliondollarmind.com

Chapter 60

Build a Financial Team

To have the best chance of retiring rich, you need to become your own Chief Financial Officer. In our decades of interviewing, consulting and observing the self-made rich, most of them have at least one thing in common: they are in control of their money. They know how much they have, where it is, and exactly how it's performing. This flies in the face of the conventional wisdom you'll hear from some experts who would prefer that you turn everything over to them. This makes it easier for them to manage, but it makes you vulnerable.

We recommend investing the time and effort required to take control of your own money and retirement. Once you assume the role of Chief Financial Officer, begin building a team of niche investment experts that can guide you and offer ideas and advice. It's one thing to ask for help when you have foundational understanding of how an investment works, and quite another when you are asking people for help on blind faith. This is too big of a deal to trust other people to always act in your best interests. You are in a race against time, and if you get bad advice, sloppy suggestions, or even ripped off, you can't get this time back. This means struggling financially for the rest of your life, especially as you move into your twilight years.

Get referrals from the most successful people you know and trust. Ask the richest people around you from whom they take advice, and make an appointment to speak with them. They're a lot of good advisors out there, but you need to vet them carefully to find which one is right for you.

> "Unity is strength... when there is teamwork and collaboration, wonderful things can be achieved."
>
> — *Mattie Stepanek*

CRITICAL THINKING QUESTION

Do you have the right financial team in place?

ACTION STEP

Analyze the efforts of your current financial team and decide if you need to make any changes.

Chapter 61

Study Personal Development

One of the most underutilized strategies of retiring rich is personal development. Your psychological, emotional and mental strength is central to your success. A test of your strength is whether or not you believe you can retire rich. Most people don't, which is one of the reasons they struggle with money their entire lives. When you don't believe you can do something, you don't take action towards it.

Studying personal development will walk you down the path of discovering the vast potential of your mind. Success principles are simple, yet the results they can generate are substantial. Studying success makes you realize the ultimate irony of the subject, which is that it's you against you. That it's all an inside job. Or at least the majority of it. The objective reality is that success is not as much about beating someone else as it is about mastering your own mind. This includes examining everything you've been told about the world, life and your place in it.

These core beliefs drive our decisions, and most of them were learned from people who were barely surviving. Many of the things we believe to be true are only partially true or not true at all. If you see this as hyperbole, dial back to the days of segregation and the belief that the color of your skin determined your worth as a human being. When a fringe faction believes that black people are not good enough to share the same water fountain, we write them off as ignorant. But when 250 million Americans believed this in the

1950s, you see the power of beliefs that are passed down and programmed into children.

Luckily, negative brainwashing can be reprogrammed to positive, life affirming, rich programming, and that's the very heart of what personal development is all about.

> "If you do what you've always done, you'll get what you've always gotten."
>
> — *Tony Robbins*

CRITICAL THINKING QUESTION

How much time and money do you invest each year in your own development?

ACTION STEP

Make a commitment to attend at least one personal development seminar every year.

RECOMMENDED RESOURCE

How Rich People Think
By Steve Siebold

Chapter 62

Kill Bad Debt

Just as there are empowering and disempowering beliefs, there is good debt and bad debt. Simply defined, good debt produces income or reduces taxes and bad debt makes you poorer. Cars, boats and toys that are financed are all examples of bad dept. The problem with bad debt is that it threatens to cancel out any gains you've made using good debt.

The middle class is well known for being burdened with too much bad debt, beginning with credit cards. The loan shark-like interest rates of this debt guarantee that the debtor will never get ahead. When combined with large mortgage and car payments, this debt becomes a retirement death sentence. Most experts agree that eliminating bad debt, starting with the high interest loans, is the first step to financial freedom. This is a simple strategy, yet few possess the mental toughness to follow it. This is where getting tough kicks in. Bad debt is more of an emotional addiction than an economic necessity. It's one thing to need a car and another to need a luxury car. Everyone needs somewhere to live, but home ownership can be expensive. Boats, motorcycles, vacations and other toys can cost a fortune.

Identify your bad debt and set a goal to eliminate it. If you need professional help, get it. Once you are only holding good debt and you have an active plan to leverage it, you'll be on your way to the next step in the process.

"Rather go to bed with out dinner than to rise in debt."

— *Benjamin Franklin*

CRITICAL THINKING QUESTION

How much bad debt do you have?

ACTION STEP

Commit to eliminating your bad debt in the next 1-3 years.

RECOMMENDED RESOURCE

The Money Answer Book

By Dave Ramsey

Chapter 63

Stay Tough When You Lose

Successful investing is not easy. As soon as you think you've mastered it, the market humbles you. Even the world's best investors get it wrong sometimes. It's easy to take a loss and retreat back into the security of cash. It's bad strategy, yet it happens every day.

The emotional sting of suffering a loss is often enough to derail even the most diehard investor. Along your journey to retiring rich, you're going to take some losses. It's not how much money you lose, but the way you respond to the loss itself that counts most. Getting down for making the wrong decision or trusting someone else is not an option. You must learn to take the good with the bad. Some days you win, and others, you lose. That's investing, and that's life. Winning doesn't require mental toughness, but losing does. That's why it's critical that you face your financial losses head on, and focus on lessons learned instead of money lost. This is a learned response. The knee jerk reaction to loss is self-pity, which only facilitates feelings of sadness, lack of control and apathy.

When you tell yourself to get tough, face the loss head on and move forward, it generates feelings of empowerment, self-control and motivation. In essence, it's not the response that helps or hurts you – it's the feelings that your response creates and the impact of those feelings on your future success. Investing is a full contact sport, so to speak, and to be successful means getting tough enough to be humble when you win and gracious when you lose. Always remember that it's a long-term process, and today's losses can become tomorrow's gains. When you're winning it can feel like you'll never lose, and when you're losing it can feel like you're going to lose forever.

High emotion exaggerates the severity of a problem and the significance of a payoff. So get tough, take control of your emotions and mentally prepare yourself for the next investment win.

"You've got to stay strong to be strong in tough times."

— *Tillman J. Ferreta*

CRITICAL THINKING QUESTION

On a scale of 1-7, with 7 being most, how would you rate your resilience?

ACTION STEP

Create a strategy to help you stay positive and motivated when you experience a setback. An example would be focusing on lessons learned from the failure.

RECOMMENDED RESOURCE

Go 4 It: Start Getting What You Want
By Robert Pascuzzi

Chapter 64

Use Metacognition

Metacognition means thinking about what we think about. As far as we can tell, human beings are the only animals capable of this special skill.

The significance of metacognition is its ability to transform our behavior through observation. For example, if you notice that your default response to receiving an unexpected financial windfall is wild spending, you can recognize this destructive behavior and alter it. You can reprogram your brain to automatically think about investing any unexpected money by repeatedly telling yourself the numerous benefits of this shift in strategy. Metacognition can also be used to identify limiting habit patterns, such as fear-based thinking and scarcity planning.

If you notice this pattern coming up consistently, consider the unintended consequences. For example, fear breeds more fear, and the more you feel it, the stronger it grows. This is one of the most common discoveries of the middle class. Once they tap into their metacognitive ability, they realize the level of fear in which they operate. Whether it's worrying about investments, markets, or what they'll do if this or that happens, this irrational fear erodes their confidence, and eventually, their happiness. The secret to tapping into the power of metacognition lies in your ability and willingness to exact meaningful change. This is what getting tough is all about. You don't have to snarl like Chuck Norris or bench press like The Rock.

All you have to do is be tough enough to change when it's the last thing that you want to do. It takes guts to walk away from a lifetime of mediocre, yet comfortable habits. Training yourself to think like a rich retiree requires that you believe you can be better tomorrow than you are today.

"People's minds are changed through observation."

— *Will Rogers*

CRITICAL THINKING QUESTION

Are your most consistent thought patterns moving you closer to a rich retirement?

ACTION STEP

Upgrade any limiting thought patterns that may be holding you back.

RECOMMENDED RESOURCE

The Little Money Bible
By Stuart Wilde

Chapter 65

Control Your Self-Talk

What you say when you talk to yourself will strongly influence your belief system. People of influence, especially when we're young, form our foundational beliefs. Parents, teachers, coaches, clergy, and other adults we admire have an enormous impact on what we believe to be true about ourselves, life, and the world around us. As children, we tend to blindly accept whatever these people tell us. And the younger they begin instilling beliefs in us, the more we tend to believe them. Some of these beliefs are positive and life affirming, and others rooted in falsehood, superstition and Iron Age philosophy.

The fact is that much of our upbringing involves the act of systematic brainwashing, both good and bad. Brainwashing a child to believe that being an honest, grateful, upstanding member of society has few drawbacks. On the other hand, telling a child that it's wrong to be rich and that all rich people are crooks can adversely affect a person for her entire life. Unfortunately, this is the brainwashing in which most of us are indoctrinated. The idea of retiring rich may appeal to the wealthy, but only a tiny percentage of people would ever admit it in mixed company. So is it really any wonder why 95% of the population of the richest country in the world have little or no net worth? Think about it: why would we ever aspire to attain something if we've been brainwashed to have disdain for it?

The answer is we wouldn't, and we don't. The key is to begin controlling and rebuilding your self-talk. Tell yourself every day that you deserve to retire rich, and that you're moving closer this goal. Take every positive thing you've ever heard about being rich and reprogram your belief system until you believe it.

> "Relentless, repetitive self-talk is what changes our self-image."
>
> — *Denis Waitley*

CRITICAL THINKING QUESTION

How often do you monitor your self-talk?

ACTION STEP

Start paying more attention to what you're saying to yourself and the way it affects your behavior.

RECOMMENDED RESOURCE

<u>What to Say When You Talk To Yourself</u>
By Dr. Shad Helmstetter

Chapter 66

Study Experts

The financial world is full of experts, most of who can be accessed online for free. This exposure to wall-street wizards and life changing financial advice is unprecedented. Your job is to take advantage of it and educate yourself. Watch videos, read articles, scour websites and study these guru's like a scientist. Start with big names like Warren Buffet, Ray Dalio and Jack Bogle, and work your way into the world of academia by learning from renowned economists.

The more you learn about how money is earned, grows and compounds, the more skilled of an investor you will become. Study financial gurus in equities, insurance, bonds, taxes and you'll walk away with a feel for the difference in these contracts, vehicles and instruments. Research the different opinions that independent fiduciaries have when it comes to annuities, indexing and mutual funds. You'll be surprised at how passionate these people are, whether they're in favor or opposed to these investments. In the beginning, it may appear that contradictions exist, but upon further examination, you'll see that most of them are saying the same thing in a different way. You'll also become acutely aware of when an expert is more of a salesperson than a fiduciary. Don't let this discourage you. Take it as a sign that you're getting smart enough to identify the difference. And just because broker is trying to sell you doesn't mean he doesn't have a good product, it simply means you need to know exactly what you're buying to insure it's in your best interests.

This is a critical step in your development. Investing 30 minutes a day in your free financial education will protect you from being misled, misinformed, and even taken. You'll also sleep better at night knowing that you have a foundational understanding of the investments that make up your portfolio.

> "Mentors, by far, are the most important aspects of businesses."
>
> — *Daymond John*

CRITICAL THINKING QUESTION

How many financial experts have you studied?

ACTION STEP

Make a commitment to read one book per quarter by a world-class financial expert.

RECOMMENDED RESOURCE

<u>Principles</u>
By Ray Dalio

Chapter 67

Avoid Excessive Cognition

The world in the 21st century is a vast arena of intellectual, informational and psychological bombardment. Between computers, tablets, mobile devices, television, radio and personal relationships, we are overwhelmed with far more input than we can process.

This is just a part of being alive during the explosion of the Internet and the digital information age. It's an exciting time to be alive, yet the systematic assault of ongoing, never ending messaging is no friend to our cognitive processes. As a matter of fact, the more data we must sift through, the less efficient our thinking becomes. The brain's processing system slows down due to the energy consumed by largely unimportant, superficial data that has little significance in our lives. Most people don't realize that their mental and emotional energy is being hijacked by reality television, video games and meaningless gossip. The secret to taking control of your mental energy lies in our ability to avoid information overload, say no to it, and ignore it. This can be difficult, since so much of our society is based around frivolous pursuits and hollow entertainment. You simply have to remove yourself from any environment that threatens to siphon mental energy that can be utilized in a more constructive capacity.

Psychological strategies such as meditation, floating, message, and deep sleep can create healthy gaps and spaces between incoming information. These gaps can give your mind the rest it needs to perform at its peak. This is why some of our best ideas come to us in seemingly strange environments, such as the shower, during exercise or on vacation. During these moments our minds are at rest, and this allows them to rebound from excessive cognition and create the space that we need to perform at our best.

"Focus."

— Dwayne "The Rock" Johnson

CRITICAL THINKING QUESTION

How is information overload impacting the quality of your creative thinking?

ACTION STEP

Make a conscious effort to reduce your exposure to unnecessary information.

RECOMMENDED RESOURCE

The Book on Floating
By Michael Hutchison

Chapter 68

Leverage Everything

The favorite word of the rich is 'leverage' – not in the context of debt, but in the art of using every asset you have in life as a lever to amass wealth. The average person is never taught to use this form of leverage, but it's one of the primary reasons that the rich get richer. And in order to retire rich, especially after 40, you will need every advantage you can get.

Take inventory of your assets, both the physical and non-physical. Obvious examples include the equity in your home, income-producing assets like rental property, stocks that pay dividends and businesses that produce profits. The non-obvious examples include the credibility you have in your business or career, the clout of the college you attended and the network of friends and colleagues you've established. The concept of leverage asks one foundational question: how can you use this asset as a lever to produce more money?

Make a list of every asset you have, and write down ideas and strategies you can employ to earn additional income you can convert to tax deferred retirement savings. Physical assets are the easiest place to start. If you own rental property, maybe it's time to raise the rent? Or make some improvements that will help you keep it rented. Non-physical assets are trickier, but can be as valuable or even more valuable than their tangible counterparts. For example, how can you leverage the network of people you've established to create more income? How about getting involved in a referral marketing company and presenting it to your vast list of contacts? These opportunities are low-cost and low-risk with high potential returns. The odds are that the majority of people in your network need to build their retirement nest egg as badly as you do. These are just a few examples of the dozens you can employ to speed the process of retiring rich.

"In all planning you make a list and you set priorities."

— *Alan Lakein*

CRITICAL THINKING QUESTION

Are you leveraging everything you have to help you retire rich?

ACTION STEP

Make a list of all of your most highly leverage-able assets.

Chapter 69

Don't Get Fancy

As loyal subscribers to the Wall Street Journal for decades, we understand the trap into which readers fall. You read the success stories of hedge fund managers, derivative creators and quants that strike it rich with ultra complex financial instruments that few people on the planet can even explain. There's no doubt that these people are brilliant mathematicians that have spent their lives poring over charts, graphs and computer screens, searching for new ways to make money.

We admire these people, but lets face it, they are rare. Most of us are not burdened with these numerical gifts. So our advice is that when it comes to retiring rich, don't get fancy. Keep your investments simple and straightforward. Find ways to serve people and organizations at a higher level. If you are employed, go to your boss and ask for more responsibility. Inquire as to how you can take some of the pressure off of his or her shoulders, even if you don't get a raise for doing it. Seek safety in simple financial vehicles to increase the odds that you won't lose the principle you've invested, and search for risk in leveraging every asset you have. Don't overlook the fact that, if you've over 40, you have a lifetime of experience to leverage to younger individuals and organization that would rather pay for your advice than to risk repeating all of the mistakes you've made over the past 20, 30 or 40 years. Again, keep it simple, but approach it boldly and fearlessly.

Sometimes the best money making ideas are remarkably simple, like selling all the extra stuff in your attic you've been saving for a rainy day. It's not fancy, but even an extra $1,000 dollars that you're able to invest and grow tax deferred over 20 years can become a substantial amount. Whenever it comes to earning or investing, think simple, safe and smart.

"Simplicity is the ultimate sophistication."

— *Leonardo Da Vinci*

CRITICAL THINKING QUESTION

Are you making retiring rich more complicated that it needs to be?

ACTION STEP

Map out a plan to simplify your retirement strategy.

Chapter 70

Embrace Calculated Risk Taking

One of the most valuable skills you can develop is the ability to sense when it's worth taking a calculated risk. These strategic moves are evaluated for their potential upsides and downsides. Properly executed, mixed with a little luck, these risks can produce enormous returns in a relatively short period of time.

An example would be starting a part-time business, or getting a part-time job. A simple risk assessment would reveal that the only exposure you have in taking the part-time job is the time required to fulfill your role. In the past few years, thousands of future retirees have created a solid part-time income. These activities won't produce a large amount of money in the beginning, but if invested wisely, even a small amount that's untouched by taxes and fueled by compound interest would shock almost anyone after 20 years of exponential growth. A solid, low-risk plan would dedicate every penny earned in a part-time job to your retirement fund. Imagine how much money employing this strategy could generate in 5 years? It wouldn't be enough to retire rich, but combined with other solid strategies, it could play a serious role.

For more aggressive gains, there's nothing that has more explosive potential than starting a part-time business. Evaluate your expertise, education and passions, and identify problems you may be able to solve, for which people will pay. Let's say you're a master salesperson. What product or service could you sell on 100% commission that you believe in and for which you have a passion? Every product or service must be sold, and no matter how much a company is selling, it's guaranteed that they want to sell more. Just remember that you're searching for low-risk, high return opportunities and leave the high-risk ventures to younger people who have a longer time horizon to retirement.

"Between calculated risk and reckless decision-making lies the dividing line between profit and loss."

— *Charles Duhigg*

CRITICAL THINKING QUESTION

Do you consider yourself a calculated risk-taker?

ACTION STEP

Identify one calculated risk you can take in the next 30 days to move you closer to retiring rich.

Chapter 71

Develop Sustained Concentration

Studies show that most people who retire rich never hit a financial home run. Their wealth is not the result of a windfall. Instead, it was built over many years of steady, unemotional investing. The get rich quick mentality that is so pervasive in America rarely produces millionaires. The irony is that when people do strike it rich in the lottery or Las Vegas, only a small percentage of them are able to hold on to it.

Unless you're a movie star, professional athlete or business tycoon, the true path to wealth is paved with steady action that's achieved through years of sustained concentration. This means keeping your eye on the retirement goal on which you've decided and refusing to allow the desires of the moment to derail your efforts. The ability to sustain your concentration over extended periods is a skill you build one day at a time, like a muscle you develop through repetition. Every day of continued focus enhances your ability to stay the course when your emotions are pushing you in the opposite direction. When you're investing money that you won't be able to spend for 10, 20 or 30 years, it's easy to fall into the instant gratification mode of spending. After all, there's always tomorrow, right? Well, yes and no. You only have so many years to sock enough away to be able to afford the lifestyle you desire and deserve. And the key to compound interest is time.

Therefore, in every sense, there is no tomorrow. There is only today. The good thing about building sustained concentration with investing is that this muscle grows stronger every day; especially on days where you want to spend but decide to save. That's when you know you successfully converted a good idea into a world-class habit.

> "Rome wasn't built in a day."
>
> — *Anonymous*

CRITICAL THINKING QUESTION

Do you have the skill required to sustain your concentration long enough to retire rich?

ACTION STEP

Start telling yourself everyday that you have a tremendous capacity for sustained concentration.

Chapter 72

Build Your Strengths

Every successful investor has his or her own strengths and weaknesses. We have friends and clients that focus their investment efforts exclusively in residential and commercial real estate, and they refuse to risk their money in any other sector. Other people invest in nothing but bonds, because they've spent years dissecting the bond market and that's where they feel most at home. Another, more unique group of investors, places their retirement money in alternative vehicles such as vintage guitars, rare coins, movie props and memorabilia, vintage automobiles and motorcycles, and other non-traditional assets.

There are hundreds of different areas in which to invest your money, in addition to the more traditional and common areas such as 401k's, Roth IRA's and mutual funds. The key is to focus and build on your strengths. If you've been a coin-collecting enthusiast since childhood, it would probably be wise to have a percentage of your portfolio represented in rare coins. Your passion for the investment will drive you to study it even further, and the more you understand where your money is, the easier it is to grow it.

Most of us have been told our entire lives to work on fixing and improving our weaknesses, yet this contradicts the research that shows the majority of wealthy people focus their energy on building their strengths. Lets face it: some people are good at math and others excel in English or social studies. People who love science don't always excel in sports, and some of the best athletes don't have any interest in any other area. We're all different, which means we have different interests and aptitudes. Why not focus 95% of your mental energy and physical time in areas that you possess the most passion and talent? Wherever your interests and aptitudes lie, there's an investment area to match it.

"If you do what you love, it is the best way to relax."

— *Christian Louboutin*

CRITICAL THINKING QUESTION

When it comes to planning for your retirement, what are your greatest strengths?

ACTION STEP

Start relying on your greatest strengths in saving, investing and planning, and shore up your weaknesses by hiring outside experts.

RECOMMENDED RESOURCE

Strengths Finder
By Tom Rath

Chapter 73

Be Decisive

One of the most rare qualities you'll find in people is decisiveness, or the ability to make a decision and stick to it. The root of decisiveness is confidence, and confidence can be built. The process of constructing confidence begins by making one decision at a time, and learning to make the best of that decision no matter the outcome.

The most successful people tend to make fast decisions and change them slowly. This concept was made legendary by managers at a famous Wall Street firm, who claimed behind closed doors that when they took a prospective trader to lunch during a job interview, and the candidate didn't decide on what he wanted for lunch within 30 seconds, he was automatically disqualified as a candidate. This may or may not be true, but it sufficiently makes the case that decisiveness is a quality that is sought after by successful teams. NFL quarterbacks face the same scrutiny, as they are faced with making fast decisions under mounting pressure from extra-large linebackers. Lots of football players can throw, but only a small percentage is capable of making fast decisions and executing them under pressure.

Retiring rich requires this same kind of decision-making skill, minus the linebackers. Experts and advisors can prepare and educate you on where they believe you should put your money, but in the end, the final decision is yours. The more confidence you have in your decision-making, the more decisive you will be. Your expertise in the investment on which you're deciding will help, but building the habit of bold decision making will be your best preparation. Begin practicing this everyday, even with trivial decisions such as what to order at a restaurant or which movie to watch on TV. The more decisions you make, and the quicker you make them, the stronger and more decisive you will become.

> "The speed of decision making is the essence of good governance."
>
> *— Piyush Goyal*

CRITICAL THINKING QUESTION

Do you consider yourself to be a decisive person?

ACTION STEP

Begin building your decision-making skills by increasing the speed in which you make even the most pedestrian of decisions.

Chapter 74

Don't Overreact

Markets fluctuate. Sometimes it makes sense, other times it doesn't. No one truly knows what the market will do day-to-day. Every investment is made on a best guess. Welcome to the world of investing. It can be thrilling and frustrating, and if you allow yourself to overreact to the ups and downs, you're less likely to retire rich.

The average investor buys when the market is overheated and sells when it experiences a correction. The secret is to remain calm and realize that building a multi-million dollar portfolio is a long-term process that has many highs and lows. This is not like blowing on the dice in Vegas and screaming for lucky seven. The best investors are emotionally steady and rarely overreact to their big successes or large losses. They simply monitor their results and accept what happens. The best way to mentally prepare for this journey is to see it as a long-term the process. No one losses a penny until they sell, so paper losses are meaningless in the short-term. The same applies to uncommonly large gains. No one profits until they sell, so jumping up and down about unusual gains is also a waste of time and energy.

Train yourself to be calm, cool and collected, whether your fortunes are hot or cold, because in the end, the short term has little impact on your long-term success. You may get a flat tire on your way to your destination, but once you arrive, you'll no longer care.

"Every now and then, markets behave like schoolchildren. They overreact, they run around like crazy."

— *James P. Gorman*

CRITICAL THINKING QUESTION

How steady are your emotional responses under pressure?

ACTION STEP

Practice reacting to stressful events in a calm and collected manner until you build it into a habit.

Chapter 75

Increase Your Financial Curiosity

The key to understanding the fascinating world of money and investing is to ask. Experts exist to answer your questions. The engine that drives the questioning process is curiosity, and cultivating it is simply a psychological habit you build one question at a time. The more questions you ask, the more you will learn, and the more you learn, the more curious you will become.

Most of us wait for our emotions to spring forward and create curiosity, but the best investors start asking questions long before they feel the emotional thrust to do so. Like other strategies we've discussed, curiosity is a success habit with the power to alter your financial destiny. And when it comes to understanding money, there's a lot to learn. What appears on the surface to be a simple, straightforward subject is actually one of the most complex areas of life. The more you learn, the more you realize how much you don't know. Ask the average investor to explain the concept of compound interest, and most will get it wrong. And once you understand it, you'll realize why some financial gurus refer to it as the 8th wonder of the world. Mutual funds also seem simple, but asking questions about the location and fees attached will show you the difference between one that creates a solid return and those that will erode any returns you realize.

Start building your curiosity muscle by making a list of questions to ask your advisor, banker or other member of your retirement team. Every answer you receive will generate additional questions, and your list of questions will grow longer, more specific, and more valuable.

> "The art and science of asking questions is the source of all knowledge."
>
> — *Thomas Berger*

CRITICAL THINKING QUESTION

On a scale of 1-7, with 7 being most curious, how curious are you when it comes to learning new ways to help you retire rich?

ACTION STEP

Start asking experts more questions about anything related to your retirement as if you were an investigative reporter researching a story.

Chapter 76

Maintain a Sense of Urgency

Do you remember hearing about retirement when you were a kid? Did you ever meet anyone who was retired, or attend a retirement party because your parents brought you along? Odds are during the course of your childhood that you encountered retirees. When you did, do you remember how old these people seemed?

Now fast-forward to the present day, and you're reading a book called Get Tough, Retire Rich. You may be many years from retirement, but it's close enough to be thinking about it. Now just for a moment, consider how long it's been since you heard the word 'retirement' as a child. I can remember hearing about my grandfather retiring, and that was in 1969. That's a half century ago, yet it seems like yesterday.

Our point is that time goes by quickly, especially when you're busy working, raising a family and leading a busy life. And the older you get, the faster time seems to go. Your retirement days are right around the corner, even if it doesn't feel like it. Like it or not, retiring rich is a time sensitive opportunity that will end someday. And when that day comes, you will have succeeded or failed.

That's why it's critical that you develop a keen sense of urgency when it comes to building your portfolio. Wake up every day as if it were your last chance to contribute to the investments you and your team have decided upon. Don't allow yourself to slip into the lazy thinking of the masses.

Many of these people are convinced that they are magically going to retire with enough money for 30 or 40 years. As a serious investor that's going to retire rich, this is a delusion you cannot afford.

"Urgency creates decision making."

— *Kevin Brady*

CRITICAL THINKING QUESTION

On a scale of 1-7, with 7 being most urgent, rate your sense of urgency as it relates to building your retirement.

ACTION STEP

If you're over 40, time is not on your side. Begin taking immediate action today to move toward your rich retirement. Even the smallest step forward will move you closer.

Chapter 77

Embrace Humor

The quest to retire rich is a tough one. You can give it any kind of positive spin you wish, but the bottom line is the same: you are in for the financial fight of your life. If this process were easy, everyone would retire with millions of dollars. They don't. And that's why you must fortify yourself for the fight. Among other things, this should include developing a sense of humor.

You might be surprised that we would reference humor in a book about retiring rich, but it's one of the most powerful psychological tools you can employ. I (Steve) often jokes with audiences that before the economy crashed in 2008, my wife and I thought we were brilliant waterfront property investors. We were making money hand over fist until the music stopped, in which time we found ourselves sitting on millions of dollars of property we couldn't sell. We went from being real estate geniuses to real estate morons. After three years of declining values, we sold most of it at 50% of its value. Not a good strategy! We lost millions, but instead of whining about it, we decided to build it into our speeches, TV and radio appearances, and even our social life. We made fun of how naïve we were, and how we should have seen the signs of the credit crash coming.

Truthfully, none of our buddies on Wall Street saw it coming either. It took almost all of us by surprise. But our decision to use this cautionary tale as an opportunity to allow people to laugh at us was one of our best decisions.

It took some sting out of the losses. Humor has the power to put things in perspective. Use it regularly to help you lighten up, and realize that no matter how bad it gets, you will survive.

"Lighten up, just enjoy life, smile more, laugh more, and don't get so worked up about things."

— *Kenneth Branagh*

CRITICAL THINKING QUESTION

How often do you use humor?

> **ACTION STEP**
>
> Make a commitment to inject more humor into your life and see the impact it has on your attitude and happiness.

Chapter 78

Go All In

Retiring rich is not what you would refer to as a passive play. As a matter of fact, it may be the most difficult thing you ever do. It will require every bit of commitment you can muster, and every ounce of discipline you have. This may seem obvious if you've been in the game for a while, but only a small percentage of people treat it with the respect it deserves and requires.

Most people approach their retirement, at least in the early years, like a hobby. In mental toughness training, we have a saying about this: "if you want a hobby, start a stamp collection. If you want to retire rich, you must go all in." Going all in means giving the goal everything you've got. It means sacrificing today's toys for tomorrow's retirement. It means following the steps we've outlined in this book to the letter, whether you feel like it or not. It means controlling urges to purchase things you don't need in order to impress people you don't like.

Going all in is easy to say, but you'll feel less enthusiastic when you arrive at the crossroads of spending versus saving. It's like building a business at the same time all of your friends are landing high paying jobs. I (Steve) can remember driving around in a beat up 1968 Oldsmobile Delta 88 that leaked gas so badly it was illegal to drive. We were building our business and reinvesting whatever profits we made back into the business. Meanwhile, our friends were going on fancy vacations, buying homes and having babies, and we couldn't even afford to pay cash for dinner. But we had decided to go all in, and we gave ourselves no choice but to succeed. It wasn't always fun, but after years of skimping, struggling and working 14 hours a day, the tide turned and the results we're overwhelming, just as we had dreamed. Going all in doesn't guarantee that you'll retire rich, but it's going to give you the best chance you'll ever have.

"Go for it now. The future is promised to no one."

— *Wayne Dyer*

CRITICAL THINKING QUESTION

If you were on trial for being fully committed to retiring rich, would there be enough evidence to convict you?

ACTION STEP

Determine what you would have to do to go all-in on your retirement plan.

Chapter 79

Sell, Baby, Sell!

If you are a well-paid professional and you have the opportunity to continue to earn a substantial salary into your 60s and 70s, then you should probably take advantage of it and save or invest every dollar. But if you're like most people who corporate America puts out to pasture in their 50s, I recommend that you learn how to sell.

Professional selling is arguably the highest paid, least understood profession in the world. The stereotypical salesperson, with which we are all too familiar, is more of an order taker than a salesperson. Selling is both an art and a science, and if you can become a master of the process, you can sell anything. There are numerous world-class sales training programs you can enroll in through live seminars or online training, so we won't attempt to conduct training here. The bottom line is that if you can sell, you will always be able to support yourself, as long as you're healthy enough to do it. The better salesperson you become, the higher-end product you can sell. The more difficult the sale, the more effective your skills must be. Imagine enrolling in a sales training course and getting a job where 100% of your income goes directly into your retirement account. A professional sales career, even part-time, can produce substantial commissions that have the power to catapult your retirement account.

This is just another option to boost your numbers, and if you think you have the talent to do it, be sure to give it careful consideration. Lots of people in their 50s, 60s and 70s are bagging groceries and greeting customers as a way of supplementing their savings, and if this is all they are capable of, that's fine. But if you're still sharp and open to learning one of the most profitable business skills, consider selling. It may make the difference between financial struggle and retiring rich.

> "Salesmanship is limitless. Our very living is selling. We are all salespeople."
>
> — *James Cash Penney*

CRITICAL THINKING QUESTION

On scale of 1-7, with 7 being the best, rate your sales skills.

ACTION STEP

Make a list of 10 different things you'd be interested in selling.

RECOMMENDED RESOURCE

Spin Selling

By Neil Rackam

Chapter 80

Join the Five O'clock Club

There are only 24 hours in a day, yet how many of them do we waste performing menial duties or engaging in mind-numbing activities? TV, video games, drinking, social media, surfing the web and a host of other things that fail to move us closer to our retirement goals. And if you analyze it, almost all of these activities are done at night, after work.

That's why we recommend that you join the 5 o'clock club, which is an informal club that wakes up at 5am to get a head start on their day. You may be inclined to waste time at 9 o'clock at night, while sipping a few cocktails and watching TV, but when you get up at 5am, you tend not to waste a single second. It seems that pulling yourself out of bed that early makes you promise yourself that it's worth the pain. So by the time the sun comes up and the world's alarm clock goes off, you're already 90-120 minutes into your day. Some people invest their time exercising, others mediate or do yoga, and some go straight to work. Whatever you decide, you'll be ahead of almost everyone with whom you compete. The second major benefit is that by 9pm you're getting ready for bed, which eliminates most of the worthless activities you'd be engaged in normally until 11 or 12. It's a double benefit.

Consider the mental clarity and power you will have during these early morning hours. 5am to 7am is far more valuable mentally than 9pm to11pm. In the morning you're fresh and rested, and at night, you're tired and sleepy. Give it a try and you'll never go back.

"Early bird gets the worm."

— *Proverbs*

CRITICAL THINKING QUESTION

Can you see the benefit of joining the 5 o'clock club?

ACTION STEP

Analyze whether or not joining the 5 o'clock club would be beneficial to you.

Chapter 81

Embrace Conflict

Hopefully by this point you know that you can't afford to turn over your retirement planning to just anyone. You can get all the help you need from competent, conflict-free advisors, but you must be the quarterback that makes the final decisions. This means that at times your advisors may disagree with your decisions, and conflict with them is inevitable. Now, let's be honest: most people hate conflict, and they'll do almost anything to avoid it. We're going to suggest that you take the opposite approach by not only embracing conflict, but also by encouraging it among your team.

First of all, let's establish the two kinds of conflict. The first is ego-driven, where a team member is pushing back to protect and even bolster his own ego. This level of conflict is a waste of time, and it's also destructive and disruptive. As the leader of your retirement team, you need to shut this down. Advisors and experts who are more interested in showcasing their intelligence should to be benched.

The second kind of conflict is when the team is arguing for the sake of improvement, where ego has no role. This is the level of conflict you want to embrace and encourage. Don't make the mistake of pre-maturely shutting down a results-driven conflict for the sake of peace among the team. Allow everyone to have their say, and if the conflict gets heated, allow it to continue until it becomes overheated. You can easily identify when a conflict gets emotionally overheated when it becomes personal. That's when you need to step in, but not a moment before.

Remember that when emotion goes up, logic goes down. This means that a heated conflict will produce more honest, emotion-driven feedback and ideas than calm and rational conflict ever will. So encourage conflict and it will take your teams strategy to the next level.

> "Peace is not absence of conflict, it is the ability to handle conflict by peaceful means."
>
> — *Ronald Reagan*

CRITICAL THINKING QUESTION

On a scale of 1-7, with 7 being the most, how comfortable are you with conflict?

ACTION STEP

Begin to engage in conversations that create conflict.

Chapter 82

Build Powerful Contacts

As the leader of your retire rich team, you want to build a network of powerful people who can help you achieve your goal. This includes certified financial planners, wealth managers, insurance experts, equities traders, 401K managers, financial book authors and speakers, and anyone else in the retirement industry that can help you.

You may be the quarterback of the team, but that doesn't mean you should be out on the field by yourself. The goal is to win the game, and that means getting all the help you can get. Connect with rich retirees on the Internet, attend retirement seminars conducted by independent financial advisors, and enroll in online training courses that can further educate you in the comfort of your own home. Network with expats who spilt their retirement between the U.S. and their adopted foreign country to reduce their expenses. Join meet up groups for investors. Read books on retirement planning and contact the author with follow up questions. Invest in a contact management system to track your network and maintain ongoing communication.

The larger your network grows, the more powerful it becomes and the more access you'll have to ideas, tactics and strategies. Build your network both online and off, and be sure to get face-to-face with people whenever possible. The closer your connection, the more likely your network will respond to your questions. Attending local, regional and national conferences on money, investing and retirement is another method of rubbing shoulders with power players. Set a goal to build a network of at least 100 people you can call on, even if you have to pay them a fee. Whatever time and money it costs to construct this network will yield strong returns.

> "Personal relationships are always the key to good business. You can buy networking; you can't buy friendships."
>
> — *Lindsay Fox*

CRITICAL THINKING QUESTION

Do you believe having the right contacts can help you retire rich?

ACTION STEP

Make a list of your best contacts and find a way to stay in touch with them at least once a quarter.

Chapter 83

Suspend Your Disbelief

A big part of retiring rich is believing you can make it happen, especially if you're over 40 and just starting to plan for retirement. If you haven't saved or invested much up until now, it's even more difficult to believe you're going to be able to pull this off.

Many people who've never had money would consider it impossible to retire rich. Why would you believe you could accomplish something you've never done? Especially when that something is a huge goal? To make it even tougher, why would you believe you could accomplish something in 10 or 20 years that most people never accomplish in 50 years? These are all logical, rational questions. The problem is that they predispose the idea that amassing wealth is a linear process, and for most self-made millionaires, it's not. A large percentage of millionaires struggle most of their lives, and then suddenly, strike it big in the last 10-20 years of their careers. This is easy to explain. Years of learning, growing and being in the game finally create the right opportunity at the right time, and the person cashes in. The world calls it an overnight success, but it was actually many years in the making. Overnight success sounds sexy, but it rarely occurs in the real world. Retiring rich is completely possible over a period of time, even if you're currently broke.

The secret is suspending your disbelief. You've probably spent your life like most of us, which is going it alone, with occasional input from experts. Well, this time needs to be different. You're assembling an army to help you win this war, and while you may not be capable of doing it alone, the army is more than capable. First, you must believe it's possible. Without your belief, you won't take action. So decide today to believe you and your team can do this, and that you will reject any feelings of doubt along the journey.

"In order to succeed, we must first believe that we can."
— *Nikos Kazantzakis*

CRITICAL THINKING QUESTION
What are the odds on you retiring rich?

ACTION STEP
Make a list of all the times in your life that you underestimated your own abilities.

Chapter 84

Learn to Choose

There are thousands of ways to invest your money, and they all claim to be the best. It's impossible to educate yourself on every one of them, but at the end of the day, you must choose. In essence, you have to learn to select the best investments and advisors based on your current knowledge. Learning to choose is not something we spend much time studying in school, yet it's one of the most important skills you can possess. When you're presented with one or two options, choosing one over the other is easy. When you're sorting through dozens of options, it can be overwhelming. The biggest surprise to many Americans is that they assumed their financial advisors were acting in their best interests. This is a reasonable assumption, yet it's not always the case. The fact is that approximately 90% of the advisors in America are brokers some or all of the time. Meaning they follow an entirely different set of laws that do not require them to act in your best interests. Brokers adhere to the 'suitability standard', requiring them to make recommendations they believe to be suitable – in other words, the recommendation may or may not be in your best interests. The broker's obligation is to the firm or company he or she is working for and to its shareholders, not you. A fiduciary however, follows a 'fiduciary standard', requiring him or her to act in your best interests. Therefore, you may not be receiving objective advice, even when the numbers appear to tell you otherwise.

Learning to choose is similar to learning to be decisive. It's a skill that can only be built through experience, and the more you do it, the stronger it gets.

> "A wise man makes his own decisions, an ignorant man follows public opinion."
>
> *— Grantland Rice*

CRITICAL THINKING QUESTION

On a scale of 1-7, with 7 being the best, rate your ability to choose.

ACTION STEP

Exercise your choice muscles by choosing one thing over another as quickly as possible.

RECOMMENDED RESOURCE

The 5 Mistakes Every Investor Makes and How to Avoid Them

By Peter Mallouk

Chapter 85

Consider Constructive Criticism

As the quarterback of your retirement team, you will always have the final decision on every investment. It's a big responsibility to shoulder, but if you're going to retire rich, it must be done. The best quarterbacks in the NFL have strengths and weaknesses, and the best coaches focus on their strengths and shore up their weaknesses. If you ask for their help, your advisory team will do the same. They will applaud your natural talents while pointing out your blind spots. Their criticism may sting, but you should consider it.

Objective third party experts tend to have the clearest view. While no one enjoys criticism, it's one of the most powerful learning mechanisms you can employ. That doesn't mean you should accept everything your advisors call you out on as fact, but you should at least ponder their words and consider that they may be correct. This may bruise your ego, but it might also save your retirement. The bottom line is that when your retirement day finally appears on the calendar, you either have the money or you don't. It's not a game you can do over, a business you can resurrect, or relationship you can repair. Once it's over, it's over. If the money isn't there, you could end up struggling for decades. So no matter how much the criticism hurts, you need to hear it from qualified people. The long-term outcome outweighs the short-term pain.

"The trouble with most of us is that we would rather be ruined by praise than saved by criticism."

— *Norman Vincent Peale*

CRITICAL THINKING QUESTION

Do you handle criticism well enough to embrace it when it's valid?

ACTION STEP

Ask people you respect to offer you constructive criticism in the areas of your life in which you wish to improve, and take note of how each criticism gets easier to hear.

Chapter 86

Rest Up

Leading a life-changing project with a team over a period of decades is an exhausting experience. That's exactly what retiring rich entails. It's an endurance contest with a series of strategies. It's difficult to keep the emotional highs and lows at bay when your future is riding on the outcome. The winning investments will energize you, and the losers will wear you out, but in the end, whether you're up or down, you have to continue playing the game. And a worn out, weary quarterback is a formula for disaster.

This is why getting the proper rest is critical. Think of it this way: do you really believe that the New England Patriots quarterback Tom Brady is sleep deprived during football season? No way. His rest ensures his ability to think clearly, especially under pressure, when it counts the most. After all, professional football is a business, not just a game. Many jobs are at risk within the Patriots billion-dollar franchise every time Brady takes the snap. Every elite athlete knows that work, both physical and mental, breaks down the mind and body, and rest and recovery is what restores them. It's an essential piece of the performance puzzle. This is why many of the people who have occupied the Oval Office were famous for taking afternoon naps. After all, is it prudent to have an exhausted commander-in-chief making life and death decisions?

Rest allows the mind and body to recharge, which changes the way we perceive the world. Be sure to build solid sleeping and resting habits, the kind that will help you perform at your full potential. You'll look, feel and think better, and that's an investment worth making.

> "Sleep is the golden chain that ties health and our bodies together."
>
> — *Thomas Dekker*

CRITICAL THINKING QUESTION

During an average night, how much quality sleep are you getting?

ACTION STEP

Set a goal to sleep at least 7 hours per night.

Chapter 87

Focus on the Future

In the age of immediate gratification and microwave thinking, most of us living in the first world are accustomed to getting what we want, when we want it. The days of saving up, layaway and putting off for tomorrow what you can buy today, are gone. It's no longer a part of our spoiled, undisciplined culture. After all, it's fun to buy the things you want. Carpe Diem, right? Well, that may be a good philosophy for life, but it's also the greatest threat to retiring rich. That's why it's critical that you begin to focus on the future. It's not as sexy or fun, but it's the only way you're going to secure your retirement. This means spending significant amounts of mental energy thinking about what your retirement will look like and feel like. The toys of today won't be as gratifying as the retirement of tomorrow.

While many of your friends will spend their days concerned about outliving their money, you'll be enjoying the fruits of your labor and hoping you'll live to be 100. Craft a written vision of your ultimate lifestyle in retirement, and describe how it feels. Go into great detail of how it feels to relax and revel in financial abundance, and live out the last third of your life in luxury. After you put this on paper, construct a vision board to graphically illustrate the same vision. Once you've completed these two assignments, you have effectively constructed your ideal future. Now, all you have to do is read your vision and study the board. Your thoughts will move in the direction of your dreams, and these tools will help make your future retirement more vivid.

> "You cannot escape the responsibility of tomorrow by evading it today."
>
> — *Abraham Lincoln*

CRITICAL THINKING QUESTION

How much time do you spend thinking about your retirement?

ACTION STEP

Commit to investing at least one hour per week focusing on your retirement.

Chapter 88

Avoid Middle-Class Thinking

The majority of the population, or what some refer to as the masses, have a disease we call 'middle-class thinking'. This is the level of thinking that arises from thoughts of fear and scarcity, and they are so deeply embedded in our collective psyche that they subconsciously impact everything we do. For many people, striving to become a member of the middle class is a dream. To many people, this means having a steady job, owning a home, and taking a family vacation every year.

While there's nothing wrong with this, it's not the level of thinking that will make you rich. Middle-class thinking plays it safe, while its big brother, world-class thinking, swings for the fences. And that's where you want to be. The fear and scarcity mindset may save you from making mistakes, but it doesn't offer the big life. Getting what you really want requires a love and abundance mindset that knows when to be aggressive and when to pull back. World-class thinkers are not risk takers or daredevils. They only engage in calculated risk taking, and fear rarely enters their mindset. They're playing to win while being unafraid to lose. They have the confidence to know that if they make an error or experience a bad break, they have the skill to recover.

People are not born with this level of confidence. It's something they develop from consistent success, or that they manufacture in their minds through persistent programming. Emotional creatures are capable of manipulating themselves. That's how people end up believing the unbelievable. Decide right now that you're going to become a world-class thinker, and get to work immediately on talking to yourself at that level. The more you do it, the faster you will believe it.

> "Abundance is not something we acquire.
> It is something we tune into."
>
> *— Wayne Dyer*

CRITICAL THINKING QUESTION

Are most of your thoughts rooted in love and abundance or fear and scarcity?

ACTION STEP

Every time you have a middle-class thought, immediately convert it to a world-class thought.

RECOMMENDED RESOURCE

You Were Born Rich
By Bob Proctor

Chapter 89

Expose Your Deepest Fear

Most of us spend our entire lives running away from and trying to bury our most frightening fears. We've been told to do this all of our lives, beginning with the boogey man under the bed. Ignore the fear and it goes away, or so we are told. Performance psychology tells us the opposite: it suggests that, if we expose our deepest fears, they begin to diminish.

In sports, one of the deepest fears athletes experience is choking, or the emotional seizure that can occur when the athlete becomes emotionally overwhelmed. Even professional athletes choke. One of the strategies they use to avoid choking is to admit their fear. Buried fears grow stronger in secrecy, which is why you want to uncover them, acknowledge your fear, and accept whatever happens. The typical result is a reduction in pressure and fear that the performer feels. Now consider your deepest fears when it comes to retirement. Might they include not having enough money; outliving your money, and getting sick and having to be cared for by Medicaid or some other program designed for the indigent? According to our research, these are three of the most common fears of future retirees.

But regardless of what your deepest fears may be, the process of attacking them is the same. Bring them out into the open. Refuse to allow them to hide, grow, and terrorize you at three in the morning. If you're married or coupled, share these fears with your partner and discuss the strategies you would employ to if they came to fruition. Treat them like the bully on the block by facing them head on, and you'll see that they're not as big and bad as you might have imagined.

> "If you want to conquer fear, don't sit home and think about it. Go out and get busy."
>
> — *Dale Carnegie*

CRITICAL THINKING QUESTION

What are you three deepest fears related to retirement?

ACTION STEP

Share your three deepest fears for retirement with your spouse or significant other.

Chapter 90

Bounce Back Strong

Along your journey towards retirement, you're going to make some mistakes, experience some setbacks, and get some bad breaks. It's the natural order of long-term progress. No matter how smart you are, how much you study or how knowledgeable your team, sometimes you're going to lose.

The secret is embracing failure as a catalyst for growth, which means bouncing back stronger than ever. This is not something with which you are born; it's something for which you train. And the training begins with mental preparation. Before the game even begins, you strategize as to how you will respond to both victory and defeat, because you'll encounter both many times along your journey. The victory dances are easy, as long as they don't cloud your judgment. Never allow winning to make you believe you'll never lose. You will. No one wins every time. Not even Wall Street quants working 16-hour days analyzing every market pattern. Losing is just a toll you pay on the road to riches.

One of the keys is psychologically releasing the embarrassment of failure, no matter how significant or stupid. Because even though you lost this round, you had the guts to play the game and entertain the associated risks. It's easy to criticize the players when you're sitting in the stands, but it's the guys with the guts to take the field that eventually win. Learn to ignore the naysayers and critics, because until you win the game, they will always exist. Reframe their criticism so it emboldens you, and you'll rebound faster. Eventually, you'll bounce back so fast and strong that the haters will move on to someone else.

"Perseverance is failing 19 times and succeeding the 20th."

— *Julie Andrews*

CRITICAL THINKING QUESTION

How would you describe your level of resiliency?

ACTION STEP

Make a commitment to become more resilient by refusing to harbor thoughts that dwell on any failure event you experience. Just accept the loss and move on.

Chapter 91

Be Coachable

When your goal is to retire rich, there's no place for hubris. Not only is it critical that you build a team of knowledgeable experts, but that you listen to them. It doesn't mean you must follow their advice, but only that you are coachable. It's your money and retirement, so you will have the ultimate say.

Never allow your ego or pride to become an obstacle on your path to prosperity. Make sure your advisors know that you are hearing them, and that you are carefully considering their advice. Much of being coachable is keeping an open mind to new ideas and maintaining a positive attitude. Advisors will give you more and better advice if they feel you are happy and grateful that they're on your team. They won't be afraid of offending or upsetting you with potential opportunities. Let them know how much you appreciate their dedication and service to you and your retirement goals. This may be common sense, but people go the extra mile for people who appreciate their efforts. No one wants to feel as though they're wasting their time or being ignored. Pull your advisory team in close, and build long-term relationships with the ones to which you most connect. Tell them you're eager to hear their suggestions, and that you are 100% coachable. And when you decide against taking their advice, let them know what you decided to do and why. Even if they disagree, they'll respect you for keeping them in the loop so they know what's going on and are able to recalibrate their advice based on the new strategy.

> "We have two ears and one mouth so that we can listen twice as much as we speak."
>
> — *Epictetus*

CRITICAL THINKING QUESTION

On scale of 1-7, with 7 being the best, how coachable are you?

ACTION STEP

Practice becoming more coachable by asking people questions and using active listening skills to record their answers.

Chapter 92

Develop World-Class Investing Habits

Habits are powerful. They often determine our success or failure in life. Discipline, careful planning and solid strategy are three of the most powerful habits you can develop.

Investing is no different. Successful investors, like great athletes, follow a set of core habits and rituals and repeat them. Habits such as evidence-based decision-making, extensive research, and emotional patience rank among the top of the list for successful investors. These habits reduce the risk of making mistakes while increasing the likelihood of success. World-class investing habits are developed day-by-day until they are forged in psychological steel. The wins are greeted with modesty, and the losses with humility, but the winning habits remain the same.

As you study successful investors, you'll discover their rituals. This allows them to calmly analyze opportunities with which they are presented. This is especially effective when an investment seems too good to be true. Jumping into any investment without proper vetting is a formula for failure, and your habits and rituals will serve as an insurance policy against knee-jerk decision-making. Managing greed is another key habit in this process, especially if you're ahead in your investments but behind in the years remaining before retirement. It's tempting to push your luck for bigger returns and greater payoffs, but it often comes at the risk of the principle. Temper your greed and focus your thinking on reasonable returns. Even if you're playing catch up with your retirement fund. Large returns are nice, but large losses can wipe you out. Everyone wants to hit the home run and circle the bases as the crowd chants their name, but the risks are rarely worth it. The quiet, humble, little guy that only hits singles but never loses money is a much better bet.

"Successful people are simply those with successful habits."

— *Brian Tracy*

CRITICAL THINKING QUESTION

How strong are your investing habits?

ACTION STEP

Do some research and document the 10 most powerful investing habits and begin putting them into practice.

Chapter 93

Study Investing Wisdom

Perhaps the most overlooked, understudied approach to financial education is quotations. Consider reading quotations, from Adam Smith in the 18th century to Warren Buffet in the 21st. Quotations offer distilled wisdom complied over centuries that possess the power to alter the way you approach investing. And they make easy reading without being overwhelming.

You'll get different opinions on everything. Some love equities, others say they the stock market is a casino. Some believe in Indexed Universal Life contracts as tax strategies, while others think it's smarter to park your money in other tax-deferred instruments. The list goes on. The purpose of studying quotations isn't to tell you where or what to invest – it's to give you a well-rounded, panoramic view of all things financial. Quotations won't teach you what to think, but how to think.

Quotations from credible sources are the result of a lifetime of education and experience, cleverly crafted into a few sentences. It's easier to draft a drawn out financial philosophy that it is to explain it in 50 words or less. To create these quotes, the author must possess an expert's depth of knowledge. If you'll commit to the daily study of quotations, which will only take a few minutes, you'll know more about investing in 12 months than 90% of the population.

The knowledge you'll gain will not only make you a more competent, confident investor, it will also give you peace of mind. It's comforting to know that when it comes to your retirement planning, you're not on the bleeding edge. You'll sleep better, invest with greater self-assurance and enjoy the journey to retirement. Put into investor's terminology, it's all upside with no exposure.

> "To acquire knowledge, one must study; but to acquire wisdom, one must observe."
>
> — *Marilyn vos Savant*

CRITICAL THINKING QUESTION

Do you see the value in studying the distilled wisdom of money experts from the present and past?

ACTION STEP

Read one quote on investing every day.

Chapter 94

Be Humble

Investing is an interesting pursuit, especially when the stakes are high. The titans of Wall Street are simply playing a game, like an avid golfer who takes his sport seriously. Their intensity and attitude make them appear as if their decisions can be life altering, yet the truth is they've already won before they hit the first ball or ring the opening bell. As they say in Las Vegas, they are playing with house money.

Working toward a rich retirement is anything but a game, and the stakes border on life and death. Running out of money with 20 years left to live is no laughing matter, and worrying about every penny you spend is not an enjoyable way to spend your golden years. Make no mistake: this is serious business, and the stakes are high. When you're investing to cover the needs and desires of the future, the stress and pressure can mount quickly.

This is why it's imperative that you adopt a few psychological strategies designed to help you steady your emotions, reduce the stress of the process and maybe even enjoy the battle. Humility is one such strategy, and it applies mostly to handling the times in the investing cycle when you are up, and even more so when you are way up. For various reasons, including luck, you may hit a home run and enjoy more than reasonable returns. Celebrate when this happens, because it's not the norm. If it were, every Wall Street trader would be rich, and every financial professional would have a world-class portfolio. They're not and they don't. Investing is contact sport, and markets take no prisoners.

When you're winning, be grateful and humble for your good fortune, knowing that it never lasts. Critical thinking tells us, and history confirms, that what goes up must come down. This is the objective reality of investing, and as long as you're mentally prepared for it, you'll never be shocked or surprised at the often-nonlinear, unpredictable ups and downs.

"Talent is God given. Be humble. Fame is man-given. Be grateful. Conceit is self-given. Be careful."

— *John Wooden*

CRITICAL THINKING QUESTION

What role will humility play in your quest to retire rich?

ACTION STEP

List three areas of your financial life where being more humble would serve your best interests.

Chapter 95

Monitor Your Attitude

As we've mentioned many times in this book, retiring rich is an extended process. Some days you're going to enjoy it, and other days, well, not so much.

Like any aspect of life, the attitude in which you approach your retirement journey will have an impact on your experience. It's been said by people wiser than us that the world is a refection of the attitude in which you approach it. Angry people live in an angry world. Frightened people live in a frightening world, and happy and optimistic people in a happy and optimistic world. As pedestrian as this philosophy may sound, it's psychologically congruent. We are creatures of perception; therefore, our perceptions paint our picture of our world.

Studying the attitudes and perceptions of people living in first-world countries easily proves this idea. One might think all of us would just be happy and grateful that by pure luck of the draw, we ended up being born with the winning lottery ticket. Through no effort of our own, we live a lifestyle that most of the world cannot even imagine. Retirement is a completely foreign concept to billions of people. They're not even familiar with the term. When the bulk of your days are spent avoiding starvation, retiring rich is not on your radar. The citizens of the first world are the luckiest people alive, and you would think that our attitudes would reflect our privilege. This is not always the case. We've become accustomed to getting what we want, and since few of us have experienced abject poverty, we have little to which to compare.

This doesn't mean you have to travel to a poor country in order to gain perspective. It just means waking yourself up to the reality that you are among the most fortunate people in the history of the world. If you'll bring that attitude into your investing life, you'll have more fun and find it easier to shrug off the tough days when things don't go your way.

> "Attitude is a little thing that makes a big difference."
>
> — *Winston Churchill*

CRITICAL THINKING QUESTION

When it comes to discussing and planning for your retirement, is your attitude helping or hurting you?

ACTION STEP

Make a decision to have a better attitude in every area of your life.

Chapter 96

Guard Your Energy

Strategic, long-term investing requires substantial and sustained mental energy. As in many pursuits, investing is a moving target of continuous change. The core principles of investing remain steadfast, yet the contracts, instruments and vehicles are in a constant state of flux. All of this change requires continuous study, but the less obvious impact is the psychological energy required to maintain your enthusiasm and passion in the process.

This is why you must guard your mental energy from anything that threatens to drain it. Physical energy is easier to understand. Few experts would claim that it's prudent for an NFL quarterback to put in a full days practice before the big game. Surely this would deplete his physical energy and reduce his ability to perform. That's why the coaching team protects him from any pre-game physical stress.

The same is true from an investor's perspective. When you're making money decisions that impact your economic future, you want to guard your mental energy to ensure that your mind is at its best when it's time to pull the trigger. Sloppy thinking leads to sloppy investing, just as clear thinking leads to clear investing. Become acutely aware of anything or anyone that threatens to drain your mental energy, knowing that this negative exposure could have a detrimental impact on your success. Monitor the times of day when your mental energy is at its peak. Many top investors reserve the early morning hours to make their most critical decisions. Other people choose other times for the same reason. Once you put a microscope to this, it will be apparent as to when you reach your mental and emotional peak.

"Thoughts are mental energy; they're the currency that you have to attract what you desire. Learn to stop spending that currency on thoughts you don't want."

— *Wayne Dyer*

CRITICAL THINKING QUESTION

How well do you guard your mental energy?

ACTION STEP

Raise your awareness of the times when your mental energy is at its peak as well as its valley, and schedule your most and least mentally challenging tasks accordingly.

Chapter 97

Follow Your Gut

Investing is both an art and a science. It's something you learn and something you feel. While it's ill advised to invest on feelings alone, it's wise to follow your gut instinct when arriving at your final decision.

Relying on your instincts will seem smart to some and foolish to others, but many investors believe that instincts are wiser than for which some give them credit. These primal warning signals have kept Homo sapiens alive for more than 100,000 years. They've been passed down through generations which have made them highly effective, especially when they sense danger. Investing may not be as dangerous as confronting a saber-toothed tiger, but even a bad decision can cost you a fortune. In addition to this natural protection mechanism, financial study further sharpens your instincts to make better-educated choices. The more knowledge you acquire, the less emotionally charged your natural instincts. Logic-driven instincts manifest the best results, where emotional instincts are more erratic.

The key to accessing your finely tuned instincts is to seek solitude and listen carefully to your gut. The more you rely on your inner wisdom, the more accurate it will become. If an investment seems too good to be true, it probably is. Get quiet, listen carefully and act prudently. Don't make all of your decisions based on your instincts, but consider them carefully if they're screaming at you. If your gut leads you to take risks that your logical mind deems unacceptable, double check with a trusted advisor before pulling the trigger.

> "Follow your instincts. That's where true wisdom manifests itself."
>
> — *Oprah Winfrey*

CRITICAL THINKING QUESTION

On a scale of 1-7, with 7 being most, how in tune are you with your gut instincts?

ACTION STEP

Begin paying more attention to your physical and emotional reactions to important opportunities where you need to make decisions.

Chapter 98

Don't Be Afraid of Pain

Amassing a fortune, especially after age forty, is no small task. You may move right through it, or you may suffer along the way. And while it would be nice to travel the easy road, odds are you will suffer your share of setbacks and failures. This is just part of the process that most self-made millionaires go through, and many of them see it as a badge of honor.

The worst part of suffering is often the fear of suffering, as opposed to the suffering itself. Human beings are hard wired to avoid pain, but oftentimes the fear of pain is worse than the actual pain. Losing money is painful. Making bad investment decisions can haunt you for years. But nothing seems to wear on people more than attaching fear to every action you take along this journey. Fear of loss, retiring without enough money, and outliving your savings can keep you up at night, but omnipresent fear will remove all the joy out of building your fortune. The vibrational frequency in which fear operates is a low-level, survival-based wavelength that attracts more fear-based thoughts. Therefore, fear generates fear, and suddenly your stress levels rise to an unhealthy peak.

Your best bet is to let fear go, and accept that you will suffer from time to time. Once you do, like a cancer patient that accepts the suffering that chemotherapy creates, your acceptance will reduce the fear you experience and create a sense of calm. There's true power in deciding to stare your worst fear straight in the face and boldly claim, "I will survive. I may not like it, and it may be painful, but I will survive. I will live to fight another day."

"Calmness is the cradle of power."

— *Josiah Gilbert Holland*

CRITICAL THINKING QUESTION

How much are you willing to endure in order to retire rich?

ACTION STEP

Make a list of 5 reasons you believe retiring rich is worth fighting for.

Chapter 99

Never Say Die

The game of retiring rich is like most games: it has a beginning, middle and end. It would seem as though the beginning would be the day you make your first deposit, and the last day when you retire.

And frankly, this would be an ideal situation. A percentage of people, especially the World War II generation, did exactly that. It's a low-stress, calculated approach to retirement, and if you can accomplish it, we recommend it wholeheartedly. But what if you turn 65 or 70 and miss the mark? What if you didn't save a penny until you were 50, and you hit retirement age with little to show for it? The fact is that this happens all the time. If this is the situation you're in right now, don't feel badly, because you're not alone. The elimination of pensions, rising costs in higher education and health care, and the financial responsibility of caring for elderly parents have put many people behind the retirement eight ball. Don't waste any time beating yourself up, because there's still time to turn this thing around.

The older you get, the tougher it is, but that doesn't mean it's not possible. Like they say in boxing, "a puncher always has a chance." Remember that with age comes wisdom, and that you're smarter at 65 than you were at 45.

Here's our final piece of advice: never say die. Either retire rich or die trying, but never give up the pursuit. Don't allow the naysayers to convince that you're too old to win. Rage against anyone that attempts to put you out to pasture. Keep fighting the good fight knowing that thousands of rich retirees amassed their fortunes after 40, and some after 70. You can do this. And we wish you the very best of luck along the way.

"Never give up. Don't ever give up."

— *Jim Valvano*

CRITICAL THINKING QUESTION

Are you ready to give retiring rich everything you've got?

ACTION STEP

Make a decision to do whatever it takes to achieve your retirement dream, and hold on to that decision no matter how tough it gets.

RECOMMENDED RESOURCE

Unstoppable

By Cynthia Kersey

Resources

- *Go 4 It!*
  www.RobertPascuzzi.com
- *Energizers*
  www.RobertPascuzzi.com
- *The Ravine*
  www.RobertPascuzzi.com
- *Secrets Self-Made Millionaires Teach Their Kids*
  www.secretsworkbook.com
- *How Rich People Think*
  www.HowRichPeopleThinkBook.com
- *177 Mental Toughness Secrets*
  www.mentaltoughnesssecrets.com

GO 4 IT!
START GETTING WHAT YOU WANT

There hasn't been a book written that will help you change your results if you don't first learn how to change your programming. Your paradigm is in control of you – it has nothing to do with what you know – you could be one of the smartest people in town and be getting the worst results.

I'm going to tell you like it is – if you really want to win keep reading! Until the paradigm changes, the results will stay the same.

Robert Pascuzzi

WHAT PEOPLE ARE SAYING

"Pascuzzi's no nonsense, get your hands dirty approach, is a breath of fresh air for anyone looking for an actionable plan to take their game to the next level."
Tony Robbins
New York Times Best-Selling Author

"Robert will change the perception of your whole life. You'll see how good life can be."
Bob Proctor
Master Success Coach and Author of You Were Born Rich

Pre-order your copy today by visiting
www.robertpascuzzi.com

Are you ready to
Start Getting What You Want?

GET FREE ACCESS TO ROBERT'S
"GO 4 IT!" ENERGIZERS

Join our weekday journey as we explore ways to improve all aspects of your life. Sign up and you will receive "energizer" emails from author and prosperity teacher Robert Pascuzzi. His messages are designed to inspire, educate, and show you how to begin implementing the strategies that are essential to *start getting what you want*.

"I'm going to tell you like it is... until the paradigm changes, the results will stay the same."

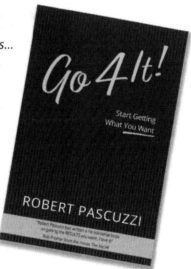

Sign up now to receive weekday
ENERGIZERS by visiting
www.robertpascuzzi.com

THE RAVINE

ARE YOU READY TO EXPLORE AND QUESTION YOUR OWN VIEWS ON FAITH, HOPE, FORGIVENESS AND THE AFTERLIFE?

On a typical weekday morning in a peaceful suburb of Akron, Ohio, the town awakens to discover that Rachel Turner and her son, Evan have been brutally murdered during the night. A short while later, Danny Turner is found in his car at the bottom of a ravine, after having taken his own life. Any explanation as to why a loving father and husband would suddenly commit a series of such heinous crimes has gone to the grave with the accused. The mystery only deepens as the details of the murders emerge, and evidence of premeditation as well as Danny's hidden past are revealed.

Subsequently, Rachel's closest friend, Carolyn Bianci, sinks into a deep depression, while her husband, Mitch, copes with his despair

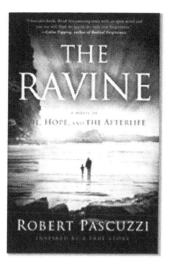

by attempting to uncover the facts of the crime. Eventually they encounter Joanna Larson, a fascinating woman who possesses extraordinary spiritual gifts. Through Joanna, the truth about the events that took place the night of the murders are unveiled. The answers Mitch and Carloyn get are beyond their human understanding.

Inspired by true events... The Ravine is currently in development to become a feature film.

Order your copy today by visiting

www.robertpascuzzi.com

Secrets Self-Made Millionaires Teach Their Kids

FREE WORKBOOK

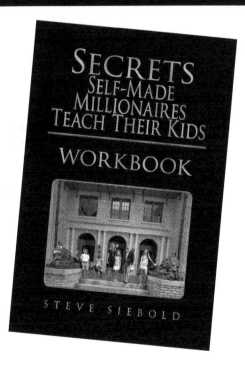

To download FREE workbook please visit:

www.secretsworkbook.com

Do You Think Like a Millionaire?

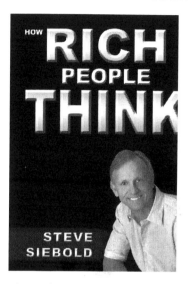

This book will teach you how. It compares the thoughts, habits and philosophies of the middle class to the world class when it comes to wealth. The differences are as extreme as they are numerous. The strategy is simple: learn how rich people think, copy them, take action and get rich This book will teach you how. It compares the thoughts, habits and philosophies of the middle class to the world class when it comes to wealth. The strategy is simple: learn how rich people think, copy them, take action and get rich. If you've ever dreamed of living a life most people only see in movies, study this book like a scientist. Freedom from financial worries and a millionaire's lifestyle is closer than you think.

How Rich People Think has been featured on ABC, NBC, CBS, CNBC and the Fox Business Network

GET 5 CHAPTERS FOR FREE AT
www.HowRichPeopleThinkBook.com

Do You Have What It Takes To Ascend To The Throne Of The World-Class?

Can a person of average intelligence and modest means ascend to the throne of the world class? 177 Mental Toughness Secrets of the World Class, identifies and explains the thought processes, habits, and philosophies of the world's greatest performers... and gives you action steps so you can implement these secrets immediately and get what you want.

People Who Adopt These 177 Mental Toughness Secrets Will Be Propelled To The Top. . .Both Personally And Professionally.

Here's What The World-Class is Saying About This Book:

"I find this book and Steve Siebold's mental toughness process to be life changing and liberating. I had a great personal and professional life before I was introduced to mental toughness. After three years of consecutive training, I have a superior life. Steve Siebold is the master of helping people prepare to win."

– Lou Wood
Region Business Director
Johnson & Johnson/OMP

"If you're interested in jump-starting a journey of personal transformation, pick this book up and dive in anywhere. It's a treasure chest of compelling messages and practical exercises. It's up to you to do the work, but Steve Siebold will point you to all the right launching points."

– Amy Edmondson, Ph.D.
Professor of Business
Administration
Harvard Business School

Order by the Case and SAVE 20%
www.mentaltoughnesssecrets.com
or call 678-971-1692

The Authors

ROBERT PASCUZZI

Robert Pascuzzi is a partner & The Director of the Corporate Retirement Plan division at Creative Planning, which has been recognized as the #1 Independent Advisor in America by Barrons Magazine from 2013-1017, and the #1 Fee-Only Wealth Management Firm in the United States by CNBC in 2014-2015.

In 2016, Forbes Magazine ranked Creative Planning the #1 Registered Investment Advisory by 10-Year Growth.

Robert personally grew the Corporate Retirement Plan division of the firm from $0 to $2.5 Billion AUM. The division currently oversees more than 1500 corporate sponsored retirement plans.

Creative Planning, based in Leawood, Kansas has approximately $35 Billion AUM and employs 750 people.

Robert has been married to wife Kelly for 25 years, and the couple has three children.

Robert has competed in 2 Iron Man competitions, and is the author of the best selling novel, The Ravine, which is currently in development to become a feature film.

STEVE SIEBOLD

Steve Siebold is an internationally recognized authority in the field of psychological performance training. His clients include Johnson & Johnson, Procter & Gamble, Toyota, GlaxoSmithKline, Caterpillar, and hundreds of others.

Since 1984, Siebold has interviewed over 1,200 self-made millionaires and billionaires, and these interviews continue today. His books, <u>177 Mental Toughness Secrets of the World Class, and How Rich People Think</u>, and <u>Secrets Self-Made Millionaires Teach Their Kids</u> have been translated in six languages and sold over one million copies worldwide.

Siebold has been featured on The Today Show, Good Morning America, CNN World News, Fox Business Network, CBS News and hundreds of other television shows throughout the country and around the world.

Siebold is the past Chairman the National Speaker's Associations Million Dollar Speakers Club, and ranks among the top 1% of professional speakers in the world.

Steve Siebold has been married to Dawn Andrews for 32 years, and the couple resides at their home/office, the historic Bona Allen Mansion, near Atlanta.

Made in the USA
San Bernardino, CA
02 June 2018